Pass the Bar Exam
with Dr. Stipkala's Proven Method

By

Jeremy M. Stipkala, Ph.D., J.D.

To Codey, my inspiration, my muse!

Persimmon Woods Press, LLC

eBook ISBN 978-0-9997997-0-3

Soft Cover Book ISBN 978-0-9997997-1-0

Table of Contents

I. Introduction

You have graduated from law school. Congratulations! You should be extremely proud of your achievement. You are joining an honored, noble, and justice-enabling profession. We lawyers are the workers and warriors who build, maintain, and defend the *foundational structure of civilization itself.*

There is just one teeny tiny little problem. You have to pass the bar exam to receive a license to do all that building, maintaining, and defending. And do not forget all the rent paying, grocery buying, and student-loan repaying that you have to do, too. That bar exam is a two or three-day contest in which you must regurgitate *everything* you ever learned in law school. And if you eventually fail to achieve a passing score, *your investment in your law school education will have been for naught.* (I vastly overstate the demands and importance of the bar exam, but you will not believe me until you **pass**.)

There is just one further teeny tiny little problem: Law school does not adequately prepare you to take the bar exam. Sure, law school attempts to teach you the law. Perhaps, law school teaches you how to think like a lawyer. Maybe even more than you care to remember, law school also exposes you to the think-on-your-feet kind of stress that lawyers sometimes endure. *But law school does not teach you how to study for and pass the bar exam!* "Really?" you ask. Yes, really, I answer. When was the last time you braved six hours of examination in a day, two or three days in a row, in a life-changing, make-or-break kind of way?

Consider running a marathon. How would you train for the marathon? You can read books and books about how to train for and run a marathon. You can watch videos, even movies, about others who have conquered the feat (feet?). But do you think that reading all the books and watching all the videos in the world about marathons would allow you to run 26.2 miles with any hope of success, or of even living through it? Dear Reader, it would be foolish and dangerous for you to read a book about running a marathon, and then go strap on some comfortable shoes and take off down the street for 26.2 miles with no other preparation.

Going further with the marathon analogy, law school vis-à-vis the bar exam prepares you to run nice little 5K and 10K fun runs. Surely a person who can run ten kilometers (six miles) is more likely to finish a marathon (alive) than a person who leads a completely sedentary lifestyle. Even so, our hypothetical fun-runner needs to train, and train differently, before she steps up to the starting line on Marathon Day.

That is what this book aims to do. Let's take smart people who have graduated law school, and teach them, *train them,* to pass the bar exam – mentally and physically. That is you, Dear Reader! Graduating from law school **proves** that you can pass the bar exam. That was a marathon of a different sort; now we will train for a new marathon since you have proven that you can run well.

Your mentor's credentials are ample. I have studied for, taken, and passed the bar exams in South Carolina, Virginia, and Washington, D.C., in addition to the United States Patent Bar Exam. In the course of those victories, I have honed my approach into a tested – *and proven* – method for passing any bar exam. I have mentored friends who have not passed the bar exam, and seen them adopt my successful method to turn discouraging failure into **magnificent triumph**. My hard-fought and hard-won achievements on those bar exams and with those friends burn inside of me, and I strongly desire to pass on what I have learned so that you, Dear Reader, can get your license to practice law sooner rather than later. If I help you to pass the bar exam, remember to pay it forward: Help some future law school graduate study for, *train for,* and pass the bar exam.

II. How to Study

A. Planning Your Study

How do you study, train, *prepare* for a bar exam? There are three essential aspects to your bar exam preparation. First, you need to internalize a considerable amount of substantive law. Second, you have got to practice, practice, practice. (If this were a marathon, you would have to run, run, run.) Third, you must manage the precious time you have to prepare. The bar exam will happen at the end of February, or at the end of July, whether you are ready or not.

Let us see how those three essential aspects combine in a suitable preparation plan. Suppose it is January 1st or June 1st, and you will take the bar exam on the last Tuesday and Wednesday in February or July. That gives you approximately fifty days to study. If at all possible, clear your schedule of every other responsibility. Take a leave of absence from your job; send your kids to grandma's for two months. If it is not possible for you to do those things, then may God bless you. You can still pass the bar exam, but it will be more demanding. (I have seen people do it – pass the bar exam while working *and* taking care of kids!) Simply put, your plan should give adequate attention to each subject, both to absorb and to practice, given the time. If you have to choose between studying and practicing, *choose practicing.* You may face a question for which you do not remember or have not studied the law no matter how much you study; later chapters will explore how to successfully attack that question. For now, know that tackling *practice test questions* will hone those skills.

First, you must determine the areas of substantive law that will appear on your bar exam. Your state bar website should list subjects that will be tested. Also, your law school will have information about the bar exam for the state where the school is. Many states (twenty-eight at the time of this writing) use the Uniform Bar Examination created by the National Conference of Bar Examiners. It is imperative that you learn early which subjects will be tested on your bar exam, so that you don't have a nasty surprise on Exam Day. These are the subjects tested by the essay portion of the Uniform Bar Examination:

Business Associations
Civil Procedure
Conflict of Laws
Constitutional Law
Contracts and Article 2 of the UCC
Criminal Law and Procedure
Evidence
Family Law
Real Property
Secured Transactions and Article 9 of the UCC
Torts
Trusts and Estates

FIND OUT **ALL** OF THE SUBJECTS BEING TESTED IN YOUR JURISDICTION *BEFORE* CRAFTING YOUR STUDY PLAN! You don't want to miss studying a tested subject, obviously.

These are the subjects tested by the multiple-choice portion of the Uniform Bar Examination:

Civil Procedure
Constitutional Law
Contracts and Articles 1 and 2 of the UCC
Criminal Law and Procedure
Evidence
Real Property
Torts

Then, of course, there is **the practical test**. Let us treat the practical test as equal to an essay subject as we develop our study plan.

(If you will take the Puerto Rico bar, then *vaya con Dios*. Louisiana bar? *Laissez les bons temps rouler!* I have no personal experience with those bar exams. However, I believe I have something useful in here for you nonetheless.)

Now that you know the substantive areas of the law that you have to internalize, make a calendar that manages internalization, practice, and time. For each day, list those subjects and tasks that you will perform. If you are studying for the bar exam without benefit of a commercial program that schedules your preparation for you, your calendar might look like this:

Day 1: TORTS. Morning: Study torts for internalization (more on how to study for internalization below). Torts are "fun" and engaging, and you probably had some idea about torts even before you went to law school. That makes torts a good place to start! Afternoon: Do a torts practice essay. Look up the law after you read the fact pattern, and keep the chapter on "Essays" below handy. Then write the essay in full. Note how long it takes. Do ten practice multiple-choice questions on torts. Look up the correct answers immediately. Then continue to study torts. Bonus: Have you made your travel and accommodations arrangements for the bar exam? Have you elected whether to write or type your essays? Attend to those matters as needed.

Day 2: TORTS. Morning: Start with ten multiple-choice questions on torts. This will get your adrenaline flowing. Continue studying torts. Afternoon: Practice essay on torts. Write out the essay in full. Do twenty multiple-choice questions on torts. Continue studying torts.

Day 3: TORTS. Morning: Start with twenty multiple-choice questions on torts. Afternoon: Do a practice essay on torts, and fifty multiple-choice questions on torts. Try hard not to peek at the law or the answers as you tackle those questions. But, once you finish the practice test, look up the model answers for essays and correct answers for multiple-choice questions and study why they are correct. Also look up the relevant black letter law in your source materials and in the study materials (outline, flashcards, whatever) that you are creating. Are your study materials effective? Is the material sticking? Are you able to internalize and then *utilize* the material on the practice questions? Finish torts today. If your elaborate outline on torts suitable for passing on to posterity is not finished yet, you need to simplify or jettison that endeavor. You've got to make your internalization efforts efficient so that you can cover all subjects.

Day 4: CIV PRO. Morning: Study civil procedure. Afternoon: Do twenty multiple-choice questions on civil procedure. Do a practice essay on civil procedure, writing your answer in full. Peek at the law and model answer as needed.

Day 5: CIV PRO. Morning: Study civil procedure. Start with ten multiple-choice questions. Afternoon: Practice essay on civil procedure – just outline your answer. Peek as needed, but try to articulate a rule of law before you peek. Do twenty multiple-choice questions on civil procedure. Continue studying civil procedure.

Day 6: CIV PRO. Morning: Start with twenty multiple-choice questions. Continue studying civil procedure. Afternoon: Outline two essays on civil procedure. Do fifty multiple-choice questions. Finish studying civil procedure.

Day 7: TEST DAY. Write out essays on torts and civil procedure, under realistic test conditions. Do fifty multiple-choice questions each on torts and civil procedure, under realistic test conditions. Immediately check the right answers for the questions you got wrong, and look up the law on each. Find the law in your source materials, and correlate the articulation of the law with the structure of the question. Say “aha!” when you see the connection! Do sets of twenty multiple-choice questions on torts and civil procedure through the afternoon. Shore up any review you need on torts and civil procedure.

Day 8: CRIM PRO. Morning: Study criminal law and procedure. Afternoon: Do twenty multiple-choice questions. Peek at the answers as needed. Immediately look up the correct answers to all questions when you have finished the twenty questions. Outline an essay. Continue studying. (I won’t keep repeating suggestions in this list calendar like: Time your practice questions; try not to peek at the answers or the law until you have made an attempt at outlining an answer; when you finish outlining/writing an essay or doing all ten/twenty/fifty multiple-choice questions, look up the answers and the law at least for the questions you missed.)

Day 9: CRIM PRO. Morning: Start with twenty multiple-choice questions. Continue studying. Afternoon: Do twenty multiple-choice questions, and outline an essay. Continue studying.

Day 10: CRIM PRO. Morning: Start with twenty multiple-choice questions. Continue studying. Afternoon: Do fifty multiple-choice questions, and outline two essays. Finish criminal law and procedure today.

Day 11: EVIDENCE. Evidence and criminal law and procedure go well together. Isn't criminal procedure ultimately about presenting evidence? Morning: Study. Afternoon: Do twenty multiple-choice questions. Peek, peek, peek. But guess first! Outline an essay. Peek at the model answer and the law as needed.

Day 12: EVIDENCE. Morning: Start with twenty multiple-choice questions. Continue studying. Afternoon: Outline an essay. Try not to peek. Do twenty multiple-choice questions. Look up the correct answers and the law when you finished with the twenty questions. Continue studying evidence.

Day 13: EVIDENCE. Morning: Start with twenty multiple-choice questions. Continue studying. Afternoon: Do fifty multiple-choice questions. Outline two essay questions on evidence.

Day 14: TEST DAY. Write out full essays, one each, for criminal law and procedure and evidence, under realistic test conditions. Do fifty questions apiece for criminal law and procedure and evidence, under realistic test conditions. Outline essays for torts, civil procedure, criminal law and procedure, and evidence. Can you get the outlines done in about ten minutes? Do sets of twenty multiple-choice questions on each of torts, civil procedure, criminal law and procedure, and evidence – keep doing sets of twenty questions, switching subjects, and looking up answers and law when you are done your twenty questions.

Day 15: CON LAW. Constitutional law goes well after criminal procedure. Morning: Study. Afternoon: Do twenty multiple-choice questions, and outline an essay. Peek freely, but guess at the answer first. Bonus: Is there anything else you need to do to be admitted to the bar exam? Has the bar acknowledged your request to write/type the essays? Have you received your registration paper that will allow you into the bar exam on Exam Day? Is it correct? Attend to those matters as needed.

Day 16: CON LAW. Morning: Do twenty multiple-choice questions, and continue studying. Afternoon: Do twenty multiple-choice questions and outline an essay. Continue studying.

Day 17: CON LAW. Morning: Start with twenty multiple-choice questions, and continue studying. Afternoon: Outline two essays, and do fifty multiple-choice questions. Continue studying.

Day 18: CON LAW. Morning: Start with twenty multiple-choice questions, and continue studying. Afternoon: Outline two essays, and do fifty multiple-choice questions. Finish constitutional law today.

Day 19: TEST DAY. Yes, have a test day after only one more subject. Constitutional law is a little bit complicated, and so bears test-driven review right after. Morning: Do fifty multiple-choice questions on constitutional law, and write out a full practice essay on constitutional law. Afternoon: Do twenty multiple-choice questions in each of torts, civil procedure, evidence, and criminal law and procedure. Do a full essay question in any one of torts, civil procedure, criminal law and procedure, and evidence, and outline an essay question in each of the remaining subjects. (That is, if you wrote an essay in torts, outline essays in civil procedure, criminal law and procedure, and evidence.)

Day 20: CONTRACTS. Morning: Study contracts law and Articles 1 and 2 of the Uniform Commercial Code (collectively, "contracts"). Afternoon: Do twenty multiple-choice questions, and outline an essay. Peek as needed. Continue studying.

Day 21: CONTRACTS. Morning: Do twenty multiple-choice questions, and continue studying. Afternoon: Do twenty multiple-choice questions and outline an essay. Continue studying.

Day 22: CONTRACTS. Morning: Start with twenty multiple-choice questions, and continue studying. Afternoon: Do fifty multiple-choice questions and outline two essays. Finish contracts today.

Day 23: PROPERTY. Contracts and real property go together well. One relates to personal property, and the other relates to real property. (When will they add **intellectual property** to the bar exam? We patent attorneys can only hope . . .) Morning: Study real property law. Afternoon: Do ten multiple-choice questions. Guess, then peek. Outline an essay, and peek, peek, peek. Continue studying.

Day 24: PROPERTY. Morning: Start with twenty multiple-choice questions. Continue studying. Afternoon: Do twenty multiple-choice questions, and outline an essay. Continue studying.

Day 25: PROPERTY. Morning: Do twenty multiple-choice questions, and continue studying. Afternoon: Do twenty multiple-choice questions, and outline an essay. Continue studying real property.

Day 26: PROPERTY. Morning: Do twenty multiple-choice questions. Continue studying. Afternoon: Do fifty multiple-choice questions, and outline two essays in real property. Finish studying real property today.

Day 27: TEST DAY. Morning: Do fifty multiple-choice questions in contracts, and then fifty multiple-choice questions in real property. Study the correct answers. Afternoon: Do twenty multiple-choice questions in each of torts, civil procedure, criminal law and procedure, evidence, constitutional law, contracts, and real property. After each twenty-question set, study the correct answers. Review the subjects causing you the most difficulty. Get a good night's rest.

Day 28: TEST DAY. Morning: Do a three-hour practice multiple-choice test on all subjects. That's one hundred randomly-arranged questions. Manage your time to get through the exam. Fill in bubbles on an answer sheet with a Number Two pencil. Be sure to mark the answer next to the number of the question you are answering! Make the practice test conditions as realistic as possible – attempt no food, water, or breaks. Afternoon: Study the right answers on the practice test. Look up the law, too. Review the subjects starting with the one you struggled with the most.

Day 29: TEST DAY. Morning: Do a three-and-a-half-hour essay test covering each of torts, civil procedure, criminal law and procedure, evidence, constitutional law, contracts, and real property, allotting thirty minutes to each subject. Make the exam conditions as realistic as possible. Use the same booklets and pens (or laptop) you will use on Exam Day. Yes, three and a half hours is more than you will endure on Exam Day. But we are building callouses here. Feel the burn. I know it sucks. But make it suck here, and it will suck less on Exam Day. Write out all answers in full. What is the quality of your essay answers? How mushy is your brain at the end? Can you read your own handwriting? How is your time management? Feel the grim joy that when you reach thirty minutes, you are done with that question. Build the discipline to move onto the next question no matter what. Battle feelings of panic and discouragement, and know that you are building the skills, knowledge, strength, and stamina to *pass the bar exam and become a real live lawyer!* Afternoon: Study the model answers to the essay questions. Review those subjects that gave you the most difficulty.

Day 30: CATCH-UP DAY. Whew. Use this day to rest, reflect, go for a walk, clear your mind. You are more than halfway ready for the bar exam! Or, if Life has been Happening to you, use this day to realign your study plan. Perhaps you needed an extra day to finish studying a subject, and so this day became your test day for essays. I suspect that you will need this day for making progress, so don't book a vacay.

Day 31: PRACTICAL TEST. Morning: Read a practical test library, peek at the model answer, and outline your response. Keep the chapter below on the practical test handy. Read another practical test library, and outline a response before peeking at the model answer. Afternoon: Do a ninety-minute practical test. How was your time management? What was the quality of your response? How close did you come to the model answer? (Note: You do *not* have to match the model answer!)

Day 32: BUS. ASSOCS. Business associations law has a certain self-consistent logic once you get into the subject. Morning: Study the law of business associations. Afternoon: Outline an essay. Feel free to peek: you are just getting into this subject. Continue studying. Bonus: Do twenty multiple-choice questions that could address all subjects. Take thirty-six minutes to do the questions, and twenty-four minutes to study the answers and the law on the questions you missed. In other words, twenty questions should take you an hour of testing and review. (Take longer on review if you need to.)

Day 33: BUS. ASSOCS. Morning: Outline an essay on business associations. Continue studying. Afternoon: Outline another essay on business associations, and continue studying. Bonus: Do twenty multiple-choice questions on random subjects.

Day 34: BUS. ASSOCS. Morning: Outline an essay to get started. Continue studying. Afternoon: Outline an essay, and then write a full essay. Finish studying business associations. Bonus: Do twenty multiple-choice questions on random subjects.

Day 35: SEC. TRANS. Secured transactions kind of goes with business associations, right? Morning: Study the law of secured transactions and Article 9 of the Uniform Commercial Code (together, "secured transactions"). Afternoon: Outline an essay. Peek if you must. Continue studying secured transactions. Bonus: Do twenty multiple-choice questions on random subjects.

Day 36: SEC. TRANS. Morning: Outline an essay. Continue studying. Afternoon: Outline another essay, then continue studying. Bonus: Do twenty multiple-choice questions on random subjects.

Day 37: SEC. TRANS. Morning: Outline an essay, and continue studying. Afternoon: Outline an essay, and then finish studying secured transactions. Bonus: Do twenty multiple-choice questions on random subjects.

Day 38: TEST DAY. Write a full essay on business associations, and a full essay on secured transactions, under realistic test conditions. Outline essay questions on each subject studied so far. Outlining should take ten minutes per question, or certainly no more than fifteen. Do fifty multiple-choice questions under realistic test conditions.

Day 39: FAMILY. Ah, family law. In real life, family law lawyers encounter humanity at its worst. Perhaps it should be called un-family law. But the horror is mitigated by at least one rule. We lawyers step in to find and enforce "the best interest of the child." That gives courts leeway to help people in distressful circumstances do The Right Thing for their kids. But I digress. Morning: Study un-family law. Start with marriage, the romantic side of family law, if you can. Afternoon: Outline an essay in family law. Continue studying. Bonus: Do twenty multiple-choice questions on random subjects.

Day 40: FAMILY. Morning: Outline an essay, and continue studying. Afternoon: Outline an essay, and continue studying family law. Bonus: Do twenty multiple-choice questions on random subjects.

Day 41: FAMILY. Morning: Outline an essay. Continue studying. Afternoon: Outline two essays, and finish family law today. (Are you a pro at internalizing and utilizing the knowledge of a subject yet?)

(I'm not saying that you should feel like God's gift to *e.g.,* family law right now, but hopefully your internalization and especially your growing ability to tackle questions should give you confidence that you are progressing *to pass the bar exam.*) Bonus: Do twenty multiple-choice questions on random subjects.

Day 42: TRUSTS & ESTATES. Trusts and estates law follows family law well, I think. Keep it all in the family, right? Morning: Study the law of Dead People and Their Stuff. Afternoon: Outline an essay, and continue studying. Bonus: Do twenty multiple-choice questions on random subjects.

Day 43: TRUSTS & ESTATES. Morning: Outline an essay, and then study. Afternoon: Outline two essays, and continue studying. (Do you see yet what I am doing? By having you tackle questions early, I hope to accomplish at least two things. First, the structure of the questions inspires and directs your studying. Second, by looking at questions before you have internalized the entire subject, and doing that over and over as you begin each new subject, you dispel feelings of panic when you encounter a question on an area of law you have not studied, or momentarily feel you have forgotten. You are training your brain to respond effectively when you face a question asking for seemingly unknown law.) Bonus: Do twenty multiple-choice questions on random subjects.

Day 44: TRUSTS & ESTATES. Morning: Outline an essay, and then study. Afternoon: Outline two essays, and finish trusts and estates. Bonus: Do twenty multiple-choice questions on random subjects.

Day 45: TEST DAY. Write out two full essays, one apiece in family law and trusts and estates. Outline essays in each subject studied so far. Look up the model answers and law for each essay, both the ones you wrote in full and the ones you outlined. Do one hundred multiple-choice questions that cover every subject. (Yes, that should take three hours.) Look up the correct answers and the law governing them. (By now, that should go without saying.)

Day 46: CONFLICTS. It is rare, in my view, to have a full-on essay just about conflicts of laws. Conflicts could appear in family law, trusts and estates law, and sometimes civil procedure and criminal procedure questions. Something happens in one state, and then people re-domicile, die, or flee to another state. So here is conflicts of laws at the end. Morning: Study conflicts of laws. Afternoon: Outline an essay on conflicts. (If you can't find any, make up a question. Decedent made a will in State A, has stuff in States A & B, owes money to someone in State C. Where should we probate the will?) (That one doesn't count – *I* made that one up.) Finish conflicts today. Bonus: Do twenty multiple-choice questions on random subjects.

Day 47: PRACTICAL TEST and REVIEW. Do a ninety-minute practical test. Write out your full answer, and stop after ninety minutes. You might be done with studying for the practical test! If you are, review your hardest subjects, and do practice questions – multiple choice and essay, as appropriate – for them. If not, work on your practical test problem: issue spotting, rule writing, time management, whatever it is. Re-read the chapter below on the practical test for refreshment or insight.

Day 48: TORTS, CIV PRO, CRIM PRO, EVIDENCE, & CON LAW. Morning: Review the law of torts, civil procedure, criminal law and procedure, evidence, and constitutional law. Caution: Staring at the page might not be effective review. Afternoon: Outline essay answers in those subjects. Then do multiple-choice questions in those areas. If you do not have subject-matter specific multiple-choice questions, do multiple-choice questions in all subject areas. *Look up the correct answers for the questions you got wrong.*

Day 49. CONTRACTS, PROPERTY, BUS. ASSOCS., & SEC. TRANS. Morning: Review the law of contracts, real property, business associations, and secured transactions. (Do NOT keep staring at the page if that is putting you to sleep. Outline essay questions to keep your alertness instead, if necessary.) Afternoon: Outline essays in contracts, real property, business associations, and secured transactions. Do multiple-choice questions in contracts and real property, or in all subjects.

Day 50: FAMILY, TRUSTS & ESTATES, CONFLICTS, & HARD SUBJECTS. Morning: Review the law in family law, trusts and estates, conflicts, and in your hardest subjects. Afternoon: Outline essays in family law, trusts and estates, and conflicts. Outline essays in your hardest subjects. Get a good night's rest.

Day 51: TEST DAY. Morning: Do a three-and-a-half-hour essay test covering each of torts, civil procedure, criminal law and procedure, evidence, constitutional law, contracts, and real property, allotting thirty minutes to each subject. Make the exam conditions as realistic as possible. Look up the model answers for each question after the three-and-a-half hours. Enjoy your greater stamina and considerable knowledge. Feels good, doesn't it? Afternoon: Do a ninety-minute practical test (if you feel you need to) AND/OR outline answers to essay questions in your hardest subjects. Then look up the model answers. Go for speed in organizing what you will write. Can you analyze a question and outline an answer in ten minutes, leaving you twenty minutes to write your butt off?

Day 52: TEST DAY. Morning: Do a three-hour multiple-choice test on all subjects. Make the exam conditions as realistic as possible, filling in bubbles to answer questions, and stopping when time is up. How is your time management? Are you putting the answers next to the correct numbers? Are you seeing your score improve? Isn't it wonderful?!? Look up answers to the questions you got wrong, and study why the right answer is the right answer. Afternoon: Do fifty-question timed batches of multiple-choice questions, and study the correct answers. Review any vague areas of the law.

Day 53: Travel Day. Review everything. Relax. Marathoners taper off the days before the Big Run. For lawyer candidates, tapering means light review of everything, especially the hard subjects.

Feel the knowledge coursing through your veins. Visualize success on the bar exam. Make sure you have all the paperwork, identification, clear plastic sandwich bag, pens, pencils, laptop and software, gasoline, snacks, water, medicine, etc., that you will need for entrance to and participation in the bar exam. Read and understand the directions for the essay test and for the practical test that you will take tomorrow. Know how and when you will get to the bar exam venue itself. Eat a good dinner and get a good night's sleep. *You got this!*

Day 54: EXAM DAY: Essays and Practical Test. Aim to get there early. Remember to breathe, to manage your time, and to write your answers in the right places. Afterwards, look up the law to a question or two, if you must. Then relax: your essays and practical test answers are in the bag! Lightly review the subjects for the multiple-choice test. Do no more than twenty random multiple-choice questions, just to get your mind pivoted to the new exam format. Feel all the relevant knowledge and techniques flooding back. Prepare your pencils, identification, clear plastic sandwich bag, etc., for the morning. Read the instructions for the multiple-choice test you will take tomorrow. Eat a good meal, and get a good night's rest.

Day 55: EXAM DAY: Multiple-Choice Test. Aim to get there early. Manage your time, and mark your answers next to the correct number. Check that often. Remember to breathe. Then you are done! With all of your hard work and a little Grace from Above, ***you will never have to take another bar exam!***

The foregoing calendar list is a suggestion. Notice how the bar exam happens on Days 54 and 55 – your timeline could be different by a day or three. (The foregoing calendar list aligns perfectly if Day 1 is June 1st, and June 1st is a Sunday.) The subjects are fewer than those I encountered on the South Carolina and Virginia bar exams. Build your own calendar. You will see from my proposed calendar list, however, a few useful techniques, I hope. Key among those techniques: *practice early and often!* Studying black letter law is rather boring if you have no purpose driving it beyond a vague "I-wanna-pass-the-bar-exam." An early view of the questions you will face will inform you and inspire you (initially scare the *poop* out of you) to seek effective internalization and utilization efforts.

B. Actual Studying: How Do You Get All This Stuff in Your Head?

In my calendar list, I say things like, "study for internalization" or "study constitutional law." What does that mean, to study effectively?

Knowledge is a little bit like dirt. The more you play with it, the more it sticks to you. You have got to play with the dirt that is the knowledge you need on the bar exam in ways that efficiently make it stick. Happily, you have had three or four years of law school learning how to make it stick. So go with what works. "Oh, but the bar exam is different!" you shriek. "Law school exams covered just one subject at a time. The bar exam covers everything! How am I going to get all the knowledge in the world about law in my head?!?" Let me encourage you, Dear Reader, that you have proven *beyond a shadow of a reasonable doubt* that you have what it takes to get the requisite knowledge in your head in a way that will allow you to call upon it, *to command it,* to do your will and earn you points on the bar exam. In fact, I submit to you that the unfortunate souls who do not pass the bar exam on the first attempt did not fail for lack of studying the law; rather, and this is the thesis of this book, *they failed to practice enough.* More on practice below.

How to study? Different techniques work for different people. I strongly suggest that you use several different techniques to create a multi-media approach. Read some, outline some, listen to a lecture some. Read concise outlines. Read detailed outlines. Write your own comprehensive outlines. Write your own "if all I knew about this area of the law was this little bit" outlines. (If all I knew about family law, it would be "do whatever is in the best interest of the child.") (Okay, there's more to family law, of course. But when you write your "if all I knew about this area of the law" outline, you may feel a sense of relief that you have learned something and can survive an essay question in that area of the law.) (Could you have written that outline a month ago?) Try flashcards. Whatever you do, DO NOT merely prepare beautiful, detailed outlines or other study materials in two dozen areas of the law, concluding that effort the day before the bar exam. The exam does not test you on how well you can write an outline of the law!

Please, please, please, Dear Reader, study AND practice! Study some, and practice some. I suggest that you will be more successful if you study some and practice some *each day*. You will find that your practice will make your study more efficient and more effective.

One plan you might follow is to attend or view some lectures such as those provided by Bar/Bri®, Kaplan, Inc., and others. Then that same day, attempt to practice outlining an essay question or answer some multiple-choice questions on the subject matter of the lecture.

But not everyone can afford those lecture courses. You must find source materials for the black-letter law that you must internalize, and practice questions galore. I am becoming a huge fan of the National Conference of Bar Examiners. They provide a wealth of information about their exams, from study aids, to online practice tests, to statistics on who is taking and passing the bar exam. I urge you to go to their website and poke around: NCBEX.org. They will write the bar exam you will probably take, so their materials are pretty much straight from the horse's mouth. I wish I had been aware of their resources back when I took my bar exams (insert geezer cough here). (I suspect those online materials were not available back then.)

Here's how I studied. For my first bar exam, I would attend a lecture (Bar/Bri®, huge fan) and take notes as best I could. (My handwriting is terrible.) Then within a half-hour of finishing the lecture, I would review my notes and fill in blanks in my notes, often with really good recollection of what I just heard in lecture. Or, for later bar exams where lectures were not an option for me, I would read outlines of black-letter law, either commercially-available outlines or detailed outlines prepared by friends who had taken the exam before. (If you are relying on outlines prepared by friends, get at least two of them. If one friend misses one detail, the other friend might catch it.) I made a point of reading through outlines for all of the subjects on the bar exam, even if I had attended a lecture on a given subject.

I also made an outline, but it was concise. I would take a sheet of legal paper (of course!) and write in small print those keywords that reflected the rule. I would write, for example, on my torts outline, "Negligence: Duty. Breach. Causation. Damages. Causation = Reasonably Foreseeable (minority: But For)." I would also annotate my outline with page numbers or other indications so I could look back at the original source in case my keyword outline was incomplete or confusing. Then, as the bar exam drew closer and closer, I would review my outlines, perhaps before practicing essays in those subjects. Importantly, I would also dive back into the detailed outlines in my source materials, sometimes for specific questions, and other times just for fun. (Ha. Ha.)

The key for me was that I was working with the knowledge, and thereby getting it to stick to me like dirt. Reading sometimes put me to sleep. Attending lectures helped me, but was complete by about mid-June. Avoid getting into a rut: There you are, doing something that is not really effective at getting the material in your brain, but you sure feel good that "Boy, oh boy, we sure are studying!" Try different things. And have I mentioned the need to practice?

C. Practice, Practice, Practice! (Run, Run, Run!)

Imagine that by Exam Day, all you have done is outlined the law. Or you have merely read outlines. That is the marathon equivalent of merely writing, or merely reading, a book about running. And then you have to go run a marathon! Your mind and, importantly, your body, are not ready for the task at hand. Another analogy: suppose you are taking a guitar class or a piano class, and your final exam, upon which your entire grade rests, consists of a recital. You do NOT want to show up at the recital having *only read about how to play your instrument.* No. You want to practice so much that your recital goes *flawlessly*, that it is almost anti-climactic because you have prepared, *practiced*, so thoroughly.

My Dear Reader, for successful marathons, musical recitals, and bar exams, your mind and body need callouses in all the right places. How do you get those callouses? That's right: PRACTICE.

I recall my first practice essay. I gave myself forty-five minutes to write my magnum opus, just like I would have on Exam Day (essays were longer on that bar exam). I diligently located the question at the end of the fact pattern, read the fact pattern, and outlined my answer. My essay was going to be great. But thirty minutes had passed! I began writing furiously! I had finished only half of my essay when time expired. I still recall the feeling of shock and horror I felt from that first practice essay. Happily, that happened in June, and I had plenty of time to recover. If your first essay goes the same way, do not worry. Just don't let your first essay be on Exam Day.

Early in your preparation schedule, practice answering essay questions fully. On those early essays, be cognizant of the time, but do not worry about meeting the time limit. Build speed later. Also, if on an early practice essay question, you have absolutely no clue how to even begin your answer, go ahead and peek. Peek at your source materials, outline, flashcards, what have you, to find any relevant rule of law. Peek at the model answer. If it is not inside your head, go outside your head to find the answer. "Oh!" you should say. "THAT's what this question seeks as an answer!" Study the rules of law that govern, now that you have seen the fact pattern. Study the model answer. Begin to match in your mind the fact pattern to the model answer. You should start to see, or even just feel, that when the question looks like this, the model answer looks like that.

Immediately after looking up the rules of law or model answer, outline and write your essay as if the rule of law came from inside your head. Later in your preparation, work hard to peek less and less. Write out your full answer before looking up the rules of law or the model answer. Practice this way and you will get better and better at answering questions in the time allotted.

The same goes for practical tests. On your first attempt, you may have to peek at the model answer. Immediately upon seeing the model answer, close the book and write your own answer. "Oh!" you will say. "That's what it feels like to write a correct answer." You will get better and better as time goes on. Go for speed later on, working to stay within the time allowed.

For multiple-choice questions, start off with small batches of questions focused in a single subject if you can. Do ten, for example, and don't worry about how long it takes. When you are finished those ten questions, immediately look up the correct answers for the questions you missed and work hard to determine why the correct answers are the correct answers. Also look up the answers for the questions you got right, to make sure your lucky guesses turn into honest wins supported by legal knowledge. Later, work for time. On the multiple-choice exam itself, you have one minute and forty-eight seconds, or 1.8 minutes, for each question. So do ten questions in eighteen minutes. Or twenty questions in thirty-six minutes. And then immediately work to learn the correct answers to the questions you got wrong.

By mid-February or mid-July, you should attempt multiple questions in a row, and even up to three-hour practice exams. Try two, and then four, and then six essay questions in a row. Try two ninety-minute practical tests in a row. Try one hour, then two hours, then three hours of multiple-choice tests. If your brain turns to mush after two hours of testing, find that out before Exam Day! Build that stamina! Learn what it takes to survive three hours of testing. Sure, you may be allowed to use a restroom during the three hours of an exam session. AVOID NEEDING TO DO THAT! Importantly, plan your nutrition and hydration for Exam Day so you are not fainting from hunger or thinking about dehydration instead of the finer points of apparent versus inherent agency authority.

By practicing, you accomplish several things. You train your mind to correctly process the question. You train your body to answer the question. Writing an exam for six hours a day exhausts the untrained mind and body. You build your mind and body into an efficient machine that can answer each question in the time allotted, and to complete the entire exam in the time allotted without petering out at the end.

D. Over and Over

Practice as much as you can. That means several practice essays in each subject. Some you will write out in full, to practice those essay-writing skills. But also practice only outlining, to get exposure to as many fact patterns as possible. Practice your multiple-choice questions by the thousands. Yes, thousands. You will thank me later.

It is my sense that the practical test does not need as much practice. Once you get the concept of how to answer a practical test, and you have done a few timed practice practical tests, you should be good. Spend your time instead internalizing substantive law and practicing your essays and your multiple-choice questions.

The skills you develop practicing are as important as the law you internalize by studying. The bar exam challenges you mentally and physically, and you can master it only by training your mind and body with practice.

There are several sources for practice exam materials. The creators of the Uniform Bar Examination and the components thereof offer a wealth of practice materials online (NCBEX.org), including actual past exams and model answers. And there exist several additional high-quality sources of practice materials. (Internet search: bar exam practice tests.) Seek practice questions that are separated by subject, as well as practice questions with subject matters mixed together, as they will be on Exam Day. Make sure that model answers accompany essay questions and practical tests, and correct answers, preferably with explanations, accompany multiple-choice questions. The bar exam will seem anti-climactic, because you will have seen it all before.

III. Essays

A. Introduction to Essays

The essay portion of the bar exam typically consists of six essay questions, each allotted thirty minutes, over the course of three hours. A question usually focuses on a single area of the law, but concepts and even rules of law from other areas of the law may be implicated in the question. A fact pattern presents a hypothetical situation, and then a question (or three) directs the lawyer candidate to make some determination as to the legal rights or outcome of a law suit based on the fact pattern. The collection of essay questions explores a variety of subjects in the law, from family law to business associations.

If a bar exam tested only whether you had legal knowledge, the exam might contain exclusively multiple-choice questions, perhaps. But a real live lawyer needs to analyze legal issues and reach legal conclusions using that legal knowledge. Also, the lawyer needs to communicate that analysis and those conclusions, often with the goal of persuading the reader. True, the correct answers in a multiple-choice test require at least some legal analysis. But the correct answer to any particular multiple-choice question completely hides whether it was obtained through sound legal analysis or by pure dumb luck. An answer to an essay question, on the other hand, simultaneously reveals the lawyer candidate's legal knowledge, legal analysis ability, and written communication ability.

Essay answers that have not earned sufficient points to pass the bar exam suffer, in my view, from two shortcomings. The first, largest shortcoming is that the answer does not have sufficient structure. The lawyer candidate has failed to build enough skeleton upon which to hang the muscle and organs of the answer. What tidbits of legal knowledge and legal analysis the candidate has placed on the page settle into a squishy pile that no bar examiner can credit. The second shortcoming, minor in comparison, is an apparent lack of legal knowledge. There is barely enough meat on the bones to show the lawyer candidate knows anything. I suspect that it is merely the lack of structure that stops candidates from passing, and the apparent lack of legal knowledge in the answer stems merely from the lack of anywhere logical to put the considerable legal knowledge the candidate truly has.

Let me teach you how to structure your essay answers. This is where your ability to reason like a lawyer will shine. And your vast legal knowledge will find a suitable place to emerge to the bar examiners' point-giving delight.

B. Structure Your Essay: Answer, Issue, Rule, Analysis, Conclusion: "AIRAC"

Just as human beings all have the same basic skeletal structure, every single legal issue that you address on the bar exam should have the same basic structure. You will address major issues, and you will address minor issues. Each and every issue should be addressed with the same structure. Importantly, the structure reveals your ability to think like a lawyer, or more specifically, to analyze a legal issue. The structure I propose states the answer, the issue, the rule of law, your analysis, and your conclusion. The acronym AIRAC summarizes the structure nicely.

Consider the following template:

A. The answer is X.
I. The issue is whether Y is true or false.
R. In this jurisdiction, Y is true when elements A, B, and C are present.
A. In this case, A is present. B is present. C is present. Accordingly, Y is true.
C. In conclusion, X is the answer since Y is true because A, B, and C are present.

Every essay answer that you write should conform or contain that rather formulaic structure. This is helpful on the bar exam to the extent that you do not have to invent a structure for your answer in addition to having to invent the answer itself.

Here is another way to express the AIRAC template:

A. [The answer is _______.]
I. The issue here is _____________.
R. In [your state], [the rule is __________].
A. In this case, [analyze whether the facts meet *each element* of the rule, and use all of the evidence].
C. In conclusion, [re-answer the question] ________________, because [give a reason] _____________.

Let me elaborate.

Answer. Bar examiners, clients, and judges all want one thing in particular: an answer. Accordingly, *answer the question*. Who wins the lawsuit? Can the defendant prove an adequate alibi? Does the plaintiff state a claim upon which relief can be granted? The first sentence of your answer should completely answer the question being asked. Do not write "yes" or "no," but rather restate the main question as a sentence giving a definite answer. "The plaintiff wins the lawsuit because a preponderance of the evidence shows the defendant's negligence." "The defendant cannot prove an adequate alibi because she has only circumstantial evidence suggesting she was at the movies, while direct evidence shows she was at the scene of the crime." "The plaintiff adequately states a claim for medical malpractice, since all elements of that claim are met in the present circumstances." The clue to starting your answer sentence appears most likely in the final sentence of the essay question. Look for the sentence that ends with a question mark. If none exists, look for an imperative sentence such as, "Explain why the court should not dismiss this case at the present stage of the litigation." Your answer sentence in this example might start with: "The court should not dismiss this case at the present stage of the litigation because ________." Simple, right? You have already earned a few points, just by answering the question!

Issue. State the issue to show the bar examiners that you are indeed a law school graduate. Do so in a sentence that informs that you are stating the issue. "The issue is

______." Even underline the word, "issue." Often, there are several issues raised in a fact pattern for an essay question. It is often simplest to deal with the issues one at a time. Apply AIRAC to the first, most-important issue, and then apply AIRAC to the next issue, and so on, until you have addressed all of the major issues. As time allows, apply AIRAC to the minor issues, too.

Rule. State the rule or rules of law that apply to your issue. Signal to the bar examiners that you are stating the rule by starting the sentence with, "In this jurisdiction," "In West Dakota [*i.e.,* the state in which you are applying for bar membership]," or the like. You might write just the two-letter abbreviation for your state to save you time: "In WD, [the rule of law is ______]."

What do you do if you forget the rule, or do not know the rule? *Make up a rule.* You know enough about the law, and will have internalized enough law to at least guess at the proper structure of a rule that governs any fact pattern that any bar exam question might throw at you. I have *never* regurgitated with statutory perfection the entire rule on any essay question in any jurisdiction for which I have passed the bar. In your law practice, you will research the statutes, regulations, and case law to quote with precision the latest and greatest articulation of the rules of law that govern your clients' matters. On the bar exam, however, nobody expects that kind of precision. If you jumble the wording a little bit, or even miss an element, you will not suffer too badly for it. Of course, do not forget the element upon which the question turns!

"Oh, no," you say. "I cannot make up a rule!" Where do you think rules came from in the first place? Someone, once upon a time, saw a fact pattern and sat down and *made up a rule* to govern what should happen in that circumstance. That is the whole premise of our common law legal system: we trust judges to sit around and make up rules. "It is emphatically the province and duty of the judicial department to say what the law is." *Marbury v. Madison,* 5 U.S. (1 Cranch) 137 (1803).

How do you get good at making up rules? *Practice.* Run, run, run!

Analysis. Apply the law to the facts of the question. Signal to the bar examiners that you are starting the analysis with, "In this case," or "Here," for example. Then address each and every element that you put into your rule. It is that simple.

How do you know what is an element of a rule? Look at each word and see whether it (or groups of words) creates its own item the prosecutor or plaintiff has to prove. Alternatively, look at each word or group of words and ask, "Could a defendant escape the claim by saying that word or group of words in the rule was absent in fact?"

Consider the rule: "A defendant is guilty of speeding if the defendant was driving a motor vehicle in excess of a posted speed limit." Let us find the elements of that rule. Was the defendant driving? Was it a motor vehicle? Was the speed of the vehicle excessive? What was the speed limit? Was it posted? Each of those questions identifies a separate element that must be addressed in your essay. As you practice your essay writing, and indeed on the bar exam itself, it may be helpful to number the elements as you write the rule. "A defendant is guilty of speeding if the (1) defendant (2) was driving (3) a motor vehicle (4) in excess of (5) a posted (6) speed limit." Number the elements at least when you outline your essay (*see* "Attacking an Essay Question" below).

Do not forget about auxiliary matters such as burdens of proof and standards of review on appeal, as appropriate. If necessary or useful, incorporate them into your articulation of the rule. "A defendant is guilty of speeding if *the State can prove beyond a shadow of a reasonable doubt that* the defendant was driving a motor vehicle in excess of a posted speed limit." Alternatively, work the burden of proof into your analysis. "It appears the State can show *beyond a shadow of a reasonable doubt* that the defendant met the excessive speed element given the radar gun's reading of 95 m.p.h., and the recent calibration of the radar gun." Or, more clearly: “The defendant met the excessive speed element given the radar gun’s reading of 95 m.p.h. The recent calibration of the radar gun, and defendant’s lack of opposing evidence, proves excessive speed *beyond a shadow of a reasonable doubt*.”

Occasionally, you can garner additional points by dealing with a rule followed by other jurisdictions, such as the minority rule. If you have time, it could be useful to apply AIRAC to discuss that other rule. Do it quickly, because that rule does not control in your jurisdiction.

Conclusion. State your conclusion, and give a reason. “In conclusion, the court should not issue an injunction in this case, because money damages will adequately compensate the plaintiff.” The conclusion will sound similar to the answer, and could be the same. If your answer fully addresses the question, as it should, the conclusion might even be omitted. Include a conclusion only if it adds new information (*i.e.,* gathers more points!). Re-read your answer sentence at the beginning of your essay. If your answer sentence is a bit thin, but fully answers the question, add a conclusion that includes a reason. For example, if the question is, "Who wins?" an adequate answer is, "The plaintiff wins the lawsuit." The conclusion should read, in this example, something like, "The plaintiff wins the lawsuit because a preponderance of the evidence shows the defendant's negligence."

Put it all together. Internalize the AIRAC structure and use it every chance you get in the days between now and the bar exam. "What time is it?" asks your beloved, seemingly ignorant of the mere fifty-something days between now and the bar exam, and the palpable sense of impending doom hanging in the air. Impress your beloved with your ability to structure your answer like a real live lawyer: "[Answer] The time is three o'clock. [Issue] The issue is, what is the current time? [Rule] In this jurisdiction, time is determined by the position of the hands of an accurately-set clock or watch. [Analysis] In this case, the clock on the wall shows that the big hand is on the twelve, and the little hand is on the three. The time on that clock matches the time on my smart phone, which is corrected whenever it receives a cellular signal. Accordingly, the clock on the wall is accurately set. [Conclusion] In conclusion, the present time as given by the accurately-set clock on the wall is three o'clock."

C. Issue Spotting

Okay, okay. Essay questions are not always as easy as telling the time. Answering them successfully will require you to work diligently and efficiently for the entire time allotted. Often, an essay question will ask you to balance competing interests. For example, in a fact pattern involving a contract, one party might breach, and then the other party breaches in retaliation. Who wins the lawsuit between them? Only sound legal analysis will tell. How do you decide what to analyze? Issue spotting!

A key to balancing the competing interests is the ability to identify separate issues. In the mutual-breach-of-contract example above, one or several issues will swirl around the first party's breach. Was it a breach? Was it justified? What are the acceptable remedies available to the non-breaching party? Let us suppose that the first party's breach was actually a breach, and unjustified, and the non-breaching party's remedies did not include breaching in retaliation.

Now we look to the second party's breach. Was it actually a breach? Was it justified, by the first party's breach or otherwise? What remedies are available to the first party because of the second party's breach? Does the first party lose any of those remedies because the first party breached? Look at all the issues that leap to mind, and we don't know anything about the case except that two parties breached a contract! Those issues leap to mind because we know a little bit about contract law. (If anything looked surprising or foreign in this paragraph, don't worry! By Exam Day, your mind will be brimming with legal knowledge and issues will leap off the page at you!)

Indeed, issues will leap off the page when you read the fact pattern. Any one issue could fill a chapter in a casebook. How do you manage all of those issues? You have to develop a sense of which issues are the most important – which issues are **dispositive**. Once you have dealt with the dispositive issue or issues, deal with as many further issues as you can to obtain as many points as you can. Then, when time runs out for that question, turn to the next question.

How can you tell which issues are important, dispositive, or should be dealt with first? Let me give you a fact pattern to practice your issue-spotting skills:

> One day, Shopkeeper, the owner of a consumer electronics store, was tending his store and noticed a shopper, Suspect, lingering at the display of a portable game console that retails for $1,000. Shopkeeper noticed Suspect standing there for approximately five minutes. When the suspect walked away, Shopkeeper walked over to the

display and noticed an empty box for the portable game console opened and on the floor near the display. Shopkeeper hurried after Suspect and saw suspect pulling his hand from his jacket pocket as Suspect passed the cash registers on the way out the door.

Shopkeeper yelled, "Stop!" and seized Suspect by the elbow. "What's in your pocket?" demanded Shopkeeper. "Nothing," answered Suspect, but refused to allow Shopkeeper to search Suspect's pockets. Shopkeeper led Suspect by the elbow to an office next to the cash registers, entered the office with Suspect, closed the door, and phoned police to request an officer. Shopkeeper stood at the door to the office with his arms crossed, blocking Suspect from leaving, for twenty minutes before Police Officer arrived to question Suspect. Police Officer frisked and searched Suspect, and found no stolen merchandise in Suspect's pockets. Police Officer let

> Suspect go. Suspect sued Shopkeeper for false imprisonment. Will Suspect win on his claim for false imprisonment?

What issue or issues are dispositive? In our suspected shoplifting case, it is more important that there was no evidence on Suspect's person that he attempted to steal anything. It is less important the value of the goods the shopkeeper suspected were lifted. Accordingly, the most important, dispositive issues in the shoplifting case involve the shopkeeper's actions vis à vis the suspect's innocence. Did the shopkeeper act reasonably? Did the shopkeeper injure the suspect? "The issue is whether the shopkeeper acted reasonably in detaining the person he suspected of shoplifting." Do you see that issue? Hopefully, also you can see how that issue might lead you to state a rule. "In this jurisdiction, a shopkeeper can detain a suspect for a reasonable amount of time and under reasonable circumstances if the shopkeeper has a genuine belief that the suspect has attempted to steal merchandise from the shopkeeper's store." Indeed, stating the dispositive issue should lead you to a full AIRAC outline and an essay.

Now, if you deal with that issue soundly, but you still have five minutes left, you might raise the minor issue of the value of the goods. The more valuable the goods, the more significant the crime, right? You can use this minor issue to augment your analysis of the major issue: what is a reasonable detention for a stolen electronic device worth $1,000 might not be reasonable for a stolen pack of gum. And your jurisdiction probably has a penal distinction between them – a felony for one, and a misdemeanor for the other. Use the five minutes you have left to show off your knowledge, and gain a few more points.

What does treatment of a minor issue look like in practice? It should look like AIRAC.

Some more tips on issue spotting: consider the evidentiary burdens, the posture of the case, and the standards of review on appeal. Those are likely never the major issue in an essay question, but many points can be had if you spot them and address them. Use AIRAC to address each of them that time allows.

D. All Elements Rule

Perhaps the single best tip I can give you, Dear Reader, appears in what I call the "All Elements Rule." In my personal, law school, and professional life, I have had very dramatic experiences that have lead me to articulate this rule for you.

My first exposure to the rule involved a rescue I performed as a lifeguard. A child slipped under the water in front of my lifeguard chair on the first day of summer, and I pulled him out and my fellow lifeguards and I gave him CPR and then rescue breathing once we detected a pulse. We cracked a rib, but he was breathing on his own by the time the ambulance collected him. The child was fine, ultimately, and Thank God For That!

A trial ensued. After the plaintiff rested, the judge gave me my first lesson in the All Elements Rule. Negligence requires (1) duty, (2) breach, (3) causation, and (4) damages. Here, the regulations held that a lifeguard has a duty to scan his area once a minute. I testified that I had scanned the area once every thirty seconds. (I didn't know the rule beforehand, promise!) So there was no breach of the duty to scan. But even if there was, there had to be damages resulting from the breach. The child's injuries, assuming that he had in fact lost his heartbeat (questionable because chest compressions alone are unlikely to restart a stopped heart), and along with a cracked rib, were all consistent with a lifeguard performing his duty and scanning the area at least once a minute. The Bad, Bad Thing that happened to that child could have happened within the space of a minute, so at least two elements, breach and damages, had not been shown. Case dismissed.

Okay, now back to bar exam preparation. The All Elements Rule means that you have to address all of the elements in your rule. Do this every single time, for every single rule, in every single opportunity on the bar exam. I will mention the All Elements Rule again when we talk about the practical test – it is that important. This single skill, or rather exercise in self-discipline, determines who passes the bar exam and who does not.

When you recite a rule, number of the elements in your outline. Write the rule in your AIRAC outline, and then go back and put a little number above each element. Then, when you are writing your analysis in your answer, cross off those elements that you have addressed. It is that simple.

Consider what it looks like in real life, if you do not follow the All Elements Rule. There you are, going on and on about how three of the four elements of negligence are met, for example. You rest your case, and your opposing counsel stands up and moves to dismiss. The judge immediately grants the motion to dismiss, because you have presented no evidence whatsoever that a crucial element has been met in the current circumstances.

This almost happened to me in law school. I was trying a case in my trial advocacy course that involved an allegation of armed robbery. I had gotten all kinds of testimony and evidence admitted relating to all of the elements except for the value of goods stolen. The rule was something like, "A person commits the felony of armed robbery if he forces a victim to surrender an article of value while the person displays or brandishes a lethal weapon." On the motion to dismiss after I rested the prosecution's case, the judge lectured me on the missing element of value. Sure, the victim testified that she surrendered her purse. Purses have value, don't they? No, they don't, unless you prove they do!

The judge denied the motion to dismiss, however, because my police officer witness testified as to the money that was in the purse, and the defense did not object to that hearsay testimony. (I suspect the judge also denied the motion so that the defense would have the pleasure of presenting their case and earning their grade.) Let us look at the rule again, and identify the elements: "A person commits the felony of armed robbery if (1) he forces (2) a victim (3) to surrender (4) an article (5) of value (6) while the person (7) displays or brandishes (8) a lethal weapon." Numbering the elements during your outlining will allow you to remember to address each element in your answer.

I won't tell you the times in my professional life when the All Elements Rule reared its ugly/beautiful head. But trust me – the bar examiners do not want a person cavorting about in civilized society, pretending to be a lawyer, if that person cannot follow the All Elements Rule.

E. All Evidence Suggestion

Use all the evidence in your fact pattern. I call this the All Evidence Suggestion. Just as the All Elements Rule gives you the discipline to fully analyze the entire rule of law governing your fact pattern, the All Evidence Suggestion gives you the discipline to fully analyze all the evidence in your fact pattern. Moreover, this will show a certain maturity in your analysis: you can deal with "bad facts," or with facts that do not support or even refute your conclusion. I call this the All Evidence Suggestion because it should not be adhered to as strictly as the All Elements Rule. Violate the All Elements Rule and you do not pass the bar exam. Omit reference to minor details in the fact pattern in harmless violation of the All Evidence Suggestion, and you still ace the bar exam.

One way to follow the All Evidence Suggestion is to number or circle the bits of evidence in your fact pattern. Then cross them off when you have used them in your essay. Of course, do not obliterate them, because you might need to see them again when you deal with another issue.

Be sure to raise and deal with facts and arguments that go against your conclusion. Consider the Shopkeeper and the Suspect in the electronics store. If you ignore the fact that no device was found in Suspect's pocket, Suspect looks guilty, guilty, guilty. But no court could convict Suspect because of that one little factoid: Suspect didn't have the game console on his person. By considering every bit of evidence, you avoid a wrong conclusion, such as: "Suspect will not prevail on his claim of false imprisonment, because Suspect is guilty of attempted larceny." Oops. That sentence would send up a Little Red Flag for the bar examiners. Accordingly, the All Elements Suggestion will allow everything in the fact pattern to make its way into your answer, in a coherent, organized, you-deserve-to-be-a-lawyer-darn-it kind of way.

F. Unknown Subject Matter

On the Virginia bar exam, I encountered a question addressing an area of the law that I had not studied at all. The fact pattern, in my estimation, called for the defense of entrapment. *Entrapment.*

Holy smokes! In all of my preparation, for every one of my bar exams, and in four years of evening law school, I had *never* encountered the entrapment defense. My dim awareness of that defense probably came from a childhood spent watching cops and robbers on TV. Didn't they know that I was a *registered patent lawyer?* That I won't need criminal law until my kids are *teenagers?* So what did I do? More germane, what will you do, Dear Reader, when you encounter something that you have never seen before?

You already know what to do. First, outline your answer using AIRAC. Answer the question: "The defendant is not guilty [of the charged offense] because he can prove an entrapment defense." (I apologize, Dear Reader, that copyright law stops me from elucidating the fact pattern here.) Now state the issue: "The issue here is whether the defendant has adequate evidence to prove his entrapment defense." Now *make up some rules*: "In this state, [the charged offense consists of elements A, B, C.] However, a defense of entrapment can defeat a criminal charge if the defendant can prove [by clear and convincing evidence?] that he was coerced by an authority to perform the acts constituting the charged offense. [I still have no idea if that rule is correct]." Once you have constructed a rule, finish your outline.

Analysis in your outline will be sparse, and the conclusion reiterates and adds to the answer.

Now it is time to write your essay. Follow your outline. Once you are happy with the rule that you have constructed, put it out of your mind that you have made it up. To enhance your essay and earn more points, consider elucidating the burden of proof that falls on the prosecution for proving the count, and the burden of proof that falls on the defendant for proving his defense. Line up every piece of evidence, both for and against the count, and for and against the defense.

You can use your imagination to introduce more evidence if you get desperate. For example, the defendant may bring in character witnesses to attest to his good character. And note in your answer that introducing character witnesses may open the door for the prosecution to introduce evidence of prior convictions. For another example, perhaps the defendant's wife or best friend can testify to conversations with the defendant before the sting about the circumstances leading to the defendant's arrest. (Hearsay?) A word of caution, however: be very careful to use every piece of evidence in the fact pattern before you go about suggesting additional evidence.

In my answer, I recall writing a few sentences about how every criminal conviction requires proof of an actus reus ("evil act") and a mens rea ("evil mind"). Here, because the defendant was coerced into committing the acts constituting the crime, the defendant did not have the requisite mens rea to be convicted for possession with intent to distribute. The point is that your answer must show the bar examiners that you have sufficient knowledge, analytical skill, and communication ability to serve society as a lawyer, not that you know how to memorize.

G. Attacking an Essay Question

When you are allowed to look at your essay question, first determine the question you have to answer. Typically, that is the last sentence of the fact pattern. Often, you will not be surprised to learn that it ends with a question mark. Sometimes, however, there will be more than one question that you have to answer. Usually, if there is a multi-part question, each part will have its own letter. For example, "(a) Who wins the lawsuit, if the court believes the first witness? (b) Who wins the lawsuit, if the court believes the second witness? (c) Who wins the lawsuit, if the video evidence clearly shows that the defendant was actually trying to help the plaintiff before the gun went off?" Skim through the fact pattern to ensure that there are not additional questions buried somewhere in the middle of the fact pattern.

Now that you know the question or number of questions that you have to answer, decide how much time you have. For a three-part question on a thirty-minute essay, you have approximately ten minutes per question, right? That is one way to look at it, and I will tell you that allotting ten minutes per question at least gives you a chance to fully address the questions. Consider how you would feel if you spent thirty minutes answering the first part, only to discover to your horror that there were two more parts to answer. I did this once during law school, and wrote a beautiful answer that was worth only ten points. I am sure that I got all ten points on that part, but my failure to plan ahead caused me to write very short answers for the remaining parts of a forty-point question.

But let us refine our time allotment here. You might give yourself, for example, fifteen minutes for the first part and just seven and a half minutes for each of the remaining two parts, to acknowledge that you don't have to read the fact pattern three times with the same care to answer each part. If necessary, write in your test booklet the time at which you must complete your answer to one part and move on to the next part – say, for an essay that starts at 10 AM, you write "10:15," "10:22:30," and "10:30." Concluding your efforts on one part and moving onto the next part reflects a beautiful truth of the bar exam: once your time has expired, you might never have to deal with that area of the law ever again, unless you really want to!

Now it is time to tackle outlining the first question. By all means, write out your new favorite acronym: AIRAC. But write it down the page in the white space in your test booklet, like this:

A
I
R
A
C

Next to the first A, write the answer to your question. Use shorthand if you can, and write only enough to spur you to write a full answer sentence in the answer booklet. Next to the I, write a word or words that identify the issue. Next to the R, write the rule out in full, and number the elements. This may be the only full sentence in your outline. Next to the second A, you might not need to write anything in your outline. Perhaps you will jot down an item of evidence to remind yourself to use it in your essay. Often, my outline was empty at this letter A, because my analysis during the actual essay writing was driven by the rule that I had written in full in my outline. Next to the C, write down a word or words to remind you of your conclusion.

If you spot another issue that needs to be addressed in your essay, write down another AIRAC outline. And repeat the foregoing exercise. Remember to always write out the entire rule in your outline, and number its elements. It is worth it! That way, your analysis will write itself when the time comes. If you shorthand the rule, you run the risk of forgetting an element when you are actually writing your essay.

Let me give you an example of an outline:

A – App'ant wins
I – Wr substantial evidence
R – (1) A jury verdict on (2) a question of fact cannot be reversed (3) on appeal if there is (4) subs. evid. to support jury verdict. Substantial evid. = (1) sufficient for (2) reasonable mind to (3) accept conclusion.
A – no matter if counter evid.

C – App'ant wins b/c no evidence supported jury verdict – only lawyer argument at closing.

From the foregoing outline, you can now see how the essay is going to be written – *how the essay is going to write itself!* Preparing the outline causes you to do a lot of the critical thinking that will help you write the answer. This saves you from having to do the critical thinking while you are also performing the mechanical task of writing your answer. The exception to this, of course, is in the analysis portion of the answer. But outlining in the foregoing way will allow you to conserve precious time by avoiding writing the analysis twice. There should be enough substance in your outline so that writing the analysis comes relatively easily.

Let us look at each line of the outline, so I can explain the thinking behind what is written.

A – App'ant wins: This obviously answers the question, which must look something like this: "Who wins the appeal [based on the foregoing fact pattern]?" Note that I referred to the party with the correct label. Since the posture of the case involves an appeal, the parties are no longer "plaintiff" and "defendant," but rather "appellant" and "respondent."

I – Wr substantial evidence: This shorthand should lead you to write, "The issue is whether substantial evidence supports the jury's verdict."

R – (1) A jury verdict on (2) a question of fact cannot be reversed (3) on appeal if there is (4) subs. evid. to support jury verdict. Substantial evid. = (1) sufficient for (2) reasonable mind to (3) accept conclusion: Well, those are the governing rules. It bears repeating: write out the rules in full and number the elements. Okay, I abbreviated a few words to save time. Make sure every word of each rule is represented in your outline, abbreviated or otherwise, so you do not omit any words from your rule written in your essay. The written rule in your outline becomes a mini-outline for your analysis.

A – no matter if counter evid.: There is not much need here to write out your analysis. You will stare at the rule in your outline when you write your analysis. The few words I have written will remind me of a point that I want to make that does not flow directly from the elements of the rule. After showing that each element of the rule is met in the facts set forth in the fact pattern, I will state, "It does not matter in this case that there is countervailing evidence, unless that countervailing evidence arises to the level of disrupting the substantial evidence supporting the verdict. Here, the lawyer's argument at closing provides no evidence to disrupt the substantial evidence supporting the verdict."

C – App'ant wins b/c no evidence supported jury verdict – only lawyer argument at closing: This is the conclusion, somewhat restating the answer but incorporating an additional reason that reveals that I can tell the difference between evidence and lawyer argument.

Now that your outline is done, glance at your watch. With practice, somewhere between five and seven-and-a-half minutes have gone by, out of the fifteen minutes you have allotted to this part of the question. That gives you at least seven-and-a-half minutes to write out your answer. Write for the full allotment of time you have set aside. Answer the question, AIRAC your essay, apply the law to the facts using the All Elements Rule, use as much evidence you can in accordance with the All Evidence Suggestion, and state your conclusion. Raise and handle any minor issues, and when the fifteen minutes expires, move on to the next question.

Look back at the fact pattern involving the Shopkeeper who detained the Suspect. Was it a reasonable detention, or false imprisonment? Here's what an essay might look like:

> "[Answer] Suspect will not win on his claim against Shopkeeper for false imprisonment. [Issue] The issue is whether the shopkeeper acted reasonably in detaining the person he suspected of shoplifting. [Rule] In this jurisdiction, a shopkeeper can detain a

suspect for a reasonable amount of time and under reasonable circumstances if the shopkeeper has a genuine belief that the suspect has attempted to steal merchandise from the shopkeeper's store. [Analysis] Here, Shopkeeper detained Suspect for twenty minutes, long enough for Police Officer to arrive. Shopkeeper promptly called for a police officer once he had detained Suspect in the office, so the amount of time of detention was reasonable. Shopkeeper led Suspect by the elbow to an office, which apparently did not injure Suspect. Shopkeeper detained Suspect in the office, where the Shopkeeper stood with his arms crossed blocking the door so Suspect could not leave the office. No other physical means were used to restrain Suspect. Because of the lack of injury or significant physical discomfort to Suspect, the circumstances of the detention were reasonable. The Shopkeeper held a genuine belief that Suspect attempted to steal a portable game console worth $1,000, because

Shopkeeper observed Suspect standing in front of the display of the consoles for five minutes, and then Shopkeeper noticed an empty box for such a console on the floor near the display. Shopkeeper also saw Suspect pull Suspect's hand from his pocket as Suspect walked passed the cash registers out the door. All of those facts caused the Shopkeeper to genuinely believe that Suspect had placed merchandise from Shopkeeper's store in Suspect's pocket in an attempt to steal that merchandise. [Conclusion] Suspect will not prevail on his claim of false imprisonment, because Shopkeeper held a genuine belief that Suspect had attempted to steal the portable game console, and because the Shopkeeper detained Suspect for a reasonable time under reasonable circumstances.

[Now I deal with the minor issue of the value of the goods suspected of being stolen:]

"[Answer] The value of the goods suspected of being stolen has no impact in this case. [Issue] Another issue here is whether the shopkeeper acted reasonably in light of the significant value of the portable game console the shopkeeper believed the suspect had stolen. [Rule] In this jurisdiction, it is a felony to steal, or to attempt to steal, goods worth $250 or more from a retail establishment. [Analysis] In this case, the shopkeeper believed that the suspect had placed a portable game console in his coat pocket. The shopkeeper found an empty box for the console on the floor in his retail establishment near where the shopkeeper had observed the suspect standing. The console was offered for retail sale at the Shopkeeper's shop for $1,000. The suspect had put his hand into his coat pocket, reasonably raising the suspicion of the shopkeeper that the suspect had, in fact, attempted to steal the console worth more than $250 from the shopkeeper's shop. Thus, the shopkeeper genuinely suspected the suspect was committing a felony. However, in fact, the suspect did not place the device in his pocket; at least, the device was not found in his pocket when the police officer searched him. While a more aggressive or intense detention could be viewed as reasonable by a jury given the device's considerable value and the suspicion of the shopkeeper that he had witnessed a felony, it is already shown above that the shopkeeper acted reasonably in detaining the suspect long enough for a police officer to arrive to search the suspect. [Conclusion] Because the considerable value of the console only makes the shopkeeper's action more reasonable, the suspect cannot win on his claim of false imprisonment in this case."

(Don't write "Answer," "Issue," "Rule," "Analysis," or "Conclusion" in your essay. I point them out here so you can see what AIRAC looks like.)

H. Attacking the Essays on the Bar Exam Itself

We all learned in second grade to "Follow Directions." Make sure you do that. At the beginning of each time period allotted to the essays, the exam proctors for the Virginia bar exam had us lawyer candidates hold up the colored booklets in which we were to write our answers. I recall there was a gold booklet, a salmon booklet, a blue booklet, and a green booklet. "Everybody holding up the gold booklet?" asked the head proctor. "Now shake it." A thousand lawyer candidates wondered the purpose of this exercise, their gold booklets flapping in the air. The proctor explained: "On the previous question, someone wrote their answer in the wrong booklet. **Please make sure you write your answer in the correct booklet."**

If you are color blind, fear not. The booklets were labeled with other identifying features. And if you still cannot tell, or are not certain, raise your hand and ask a proctor for assistance.

On the bar exam itself, time is your enemy and your friend. When time runs out, you are done. Make time work for you! Know the structure of your essay exam before you go into it. You do NOT want to spend precious time during the exam reading instructions – read those instructions beforehand if you can. (Exam proctors sometimes had us read the instructions before the exam started!) Get past exams and thoroughly digest the structure of the exam at your leisure. Then, quickly review the instructions when you are told to begin the exam to ensure that you are following those instructions!

I. Concise Instructions for Essay Questions

Concise instructions that synthesize all of the foregoing:

Know the structure of the exam before Exam Day.

Write your answer in the correct booklet/place.

Manage your time – know how much time you have for each essay question and each part of each essay question.

Find the question or questions you have to answer.

Read the fact pattern carefully.

Spot the issues.

Outline using AIRAC – write the rule in full and number the elements.

Write your essay. When you write the analysis, follow the All Elements Rule by ticking off the elements of the rule in your outline.

As you write the analysis, also remember the All Evidence Suggestion – use every piece of evidence from the fact pattern in your analysis.

Raise and deal with minor issues using AIRAC until your time runs out.

Then move on to the next question.

IV. Practical Test

A. Introduction to the Practical Test

The practical test typically involves a collection of documents comprising facts and law, and you have to show your ability to analyze them and deliver legal work product. That collection may be referred to as "the library." In the library, a memorandum will set forth the task you have to perform, such as writing a memorandum of law or a letter to a client. Legal materials such as statutes, regulations, and/or cases will explain the law in your jurisdiction. Additional documents such as a newspaper article may provide additional relevant information. Often, you will have to write two practical tests, each one ninety minutes long, over the course of three hours. The practical tests count for one fifth of the bar exam grade in some jurisdictions.

Know the structure of your practical test before Exam Day. Read the instructions from published practical tests so you are familiar. Then, on Exam Day, reading the instructions should confirm what you already know, and any differences in the instructions should jump out at you. Of course, make certain you are writing your answer in the correct booklet or place.

B. Determine the Task to Be Performed

If the question calls for a memorandum, and you write a letter, that is Not A Good Thing. Accordingly, there are points to be won just by performing the proper task. When you first get to your materials (wait for permission, of course!), identify the task you are to perform. It should be near the top or the bottom of the memorandum. Be careful that you do not misinterpret something that you read quickly. "Your client received a nasty letter" does not mean that your task is to prepare a nasty letter! Circle the imperative sentence that contains your task, and make sure you set out to do that task.

C. Read the Entire Library

Next, take the time to read the entire library. Carefully read the memorandum, the statutes, cases, and regulations, and all other material in the library. Circle rules of law and pertinent bits of evidence. Ignore, for the moment, seemingly superfluous stuff like, "The defendant was very angry . . .." Plenty of superfluous stuff will appear on your first read. You may come back and use some of it, so don't ignore it completely. What if your client didn't do something he was supposed to do because the defendant was very angry, and your client reasonably feared assault or decided to de-escalate the situation? Dealing with your client's actions could change a left-the-scene-of-an-accident to a left-the-presence-of-an-angry-person-once-it-was-clear-nobody-was-severly-injured. I urge you to read every word at least once – do not skim, as you might miss something important.

If necessary, read the library a second time. This time, the entire library will be fresh in your mind (you just read it carefully).

Just like watching an awesome movie a second time, you will see things that you missed the first time. Now you have uploaded the entire library into your mental RAM, and you are ready to organize your answer.

D. All Elements Rule – Outline Your Answer

Ah, our friend, the All Elements Rule, rides again to save the day! Here the All Elements Rule requires you to go on an Easter egg hunt. Some of the elements will appear in one of the statutes, regulations, or cases you receive in your library. The rest of the elements likely will be found in the next legal document. So, for example, the first case will involve a car accident, and the court will recite the rule for negligence: "A claim of negligence requires the plaintiff to prove by a preponderance of the evidence that the defendant had a duty to the plaintiff, the defendant breached that duty, and that breach directly caused injury to the plaintiff." The second case, for example, will expound on causation, or damages. "In this jurisdiction, causation requires that the damage suffered by the plaintiff was reasonably foreseeable." Or, for example, "A plaintiff can recover for foreseeable damages, but cannot recover for special damages." So you see, it would not suffice to read the memorandum and just one legal document and start outlining your answer memo or letter.

Now you are ready to outline your answer. Our other, bestest friend, AIRAC, rides again here. Let me expand on my hypothetical above to illustrate how you might outline your answer.

MEMO

A – P wins b/c injury was foreseeable.

I – Wr. negligence lies b/c injury did not directly follow D's actions.

R – "A claim of negligence requires the plaintiff to prove by a preponderance of the evidence that the defendant had a duty to the plaintiff, the defendant breached that duty, and that breach directly caused injury to the plaintiff." AND "In this jurisdiction, causation requires that the damage suffered by the plaintiff was reasonably foreseeable."

A – All Elements – All Evidence!
C – P wins.

Notice how I copied the rule right out of the two cases.

E. Write Your Answer

Go back to the instructional memorandum in the library, and confirm that you know the task you must perform. If it is a memo, write a memo. If it is a letter, write a letter. If it is a complaint, write a complaint. To whom is the memorandum addressed? We know from whom it shall come: "Attorney at Law." Do not write your name or any identifying information, obviously. Optionally, use headings to identify the parts of your document. Be sure to answer the question. "Write a memorandum advising Mr. Green whether he could successfully sue Mr. Brown in this case." In your answer memorandum, your first sentence should be something like, "It is my legal opinion that you could successfully sue Mr. Brown on a claim of negligence in a state court of West Dakota, given the facts as I currently understand them."

Following your outline, state the issue. In many ways, your answer memorandum should feel a lot like writing an essay. (Thank you, AIRAC!) Next recite the rules. Use good legal writing protocol, such as citations. For example, "A claim of negligence requires the plaintiff to prove by a preponderance of the evidence that the defendant had a duty to the plaintiff, the defendant breached that duty, and that breach directly caused injury to the plaintiff." Smith v. Jones, 123 State Rep. 456, 460 (W.D. 2021). Yes, that's right. I just gave a citation to the first case in the library in my memorandum. Show the bar examiners that you know how to do that. Do the same for any legal authority that you quote. You do not need perfect Bluebook® citation style, but show that you get the concept of legal citation. Citation information should appear in the case somewhere.

Be certain that you address every element of the rules, especially the elements from the second case in this example, in your answer, and examine each piece of evidence in that analysis. If there are evidentiary problems, such as for example a newspaper article stating facts, indicate those problems in your answer. "The newspaper article asserts that [X] is true. Although the newspaper article itself is inadmissible in court as hearsay evidence, if admissible evidence can be developed showing that [X] is in fact true, [element C of the rule] is met in this case."

Also consider auxiliary legal issues such as jurisdiction, venue, and evidentiary burdens, where applicable. Nothing in your instructional memorandum might mention the issues of jurisdiction or venue, but if a suit could be filed in court, a real live lawyer should consider such matters. A brief sentence mentioning that the court should have personal jurisdiction over the defendant brings joy to the hearts of bar examiners everywhere.

It could come to pass that a deeper analysis is required. The cases that you are given, for example, may have relevant fact patterns that have similarities to the fact pattern that you address. If you see that, ask yourself whether the bar examiners are trying to tell you something. It may be that the examiners (or authors of the exam question) probe whether you can analyze a case, and not just discern a rule of law. "In that case, the plaintiff lost because ______. In the present case, I am confident that the plaintiff will win because [the facts differ from the prior case]." What I am talking about is diving into the facts and outcome of the cases in the library, and using similarities and differences therein to predict the outcome in your case. That's what lawyers do all the time. If you see the opportunity to do the same on the practical test, go for it!

F. All Evidence Suggestion

In the analysis portion of your answer, work hard to include all of the evidence set forth in the library. Some evidence will be revealed in the instructional memorandum, and other evidence will appear in the other documents in the library. If, at the end of your answer, you have completely left out any reference to one of the documents in the library, you are probably missing something from your answer. During the outlining, look through all of the documents at your disposal and ask yourself whether you have used something from every document. There may be multiple somethings in each document, so be thorough! This is where your thorough read will assist you to avoid missing anything. When you are completing the writing of your analysis, review whether you have addressed All of the Elements of the rules of law, and used All of the Evidence, even if, especially if, there is any evidence that goes against your conclusion.

The practical test examines less whether you can issue-spot, and examines more whether you can piece together law and facts to reach a conclusion. The library will give you complimentary rules of law from two separate documents, and Big Question Number One is whether you can use rules from those two documents in your answer. Similarly, evidence and facts appear in several documents, and Big Question Number Two is whether you can reach a sound legal conclusion based on ALL of the facts, not just those few facts that strongly support your conclusion. In your essays (see previous chapter), the bar examiners are looking for issue-spotting skills. In the practical test, the bar examiners want to see if you can handle a constellation of facts. The All Evidence Suggestion should help you consider all of the evidence, and communicate to the bar examiners that you have.

G. Manage Your Time

You should spend about thirty minutes reading the library and outlining your answer. Then spend the rest of the time writing your answer, addressing all of the elements with all of the evidence.

If organizing your answer takes more than about one-third of the time allotted, determine what is slowing you down. Is it locating the task to be performed? Is it determining the rules of law governing your task? Is it reading? If you can spot the slow step, work on that.

In my experience, reading the library takes the longest time. At first, you have a large collection of documents, initially no idea of what you are supposed to do, and the clock is ticking. Take a deep breath, and calm yourself. How do you run a marathon? One step at a time. If necessary, in practice, say aloud the act or chore you are performing, to focus your efforts. "I am looking for the rules of law that govern." Once you have read the library, it should be fairly easy to find those rules again. Importantly, do not let your mind get distracted, for example, by a key piece of evidence that you did not notice before, when you are focused on the chore of locating the rules of law. My point here is that the practical test takes discipline, rather than grand legal knowledge. Do one chore, and then do the next. Left, right, left, right, wins a marathon. As you practice, work to focus on one chore at a time. Then, work to get your organizing done in about one third of the time allotted, to leave you two-thirds of the time to write your answer.

During the DC bar exam, which included a practical test, I sat at a table with another lawyer candidate. Before the practical test, she told me that she had taken the bar exam three times before. I wished her luck, and silently prayed desperately for us both, my confidence shaken. Well, I launched into the practical test, read everything, outlined my answer memorandum, and was scribbling away. Over an hour into the test, I realized that I was doing well and was perhaps a bit ahead of schedule. I paused in my writing, and I allowed my consciousness, my awareness, to expand to take in the sounds and atmosphere of the room. I was taking my first bar exam, and doing well – so far so good! Well, I did not dare take my eyes off my page, lest the exam proctor suspect I was peeking at anyone else's answer. But I could hear, all across the room, the sound of furious scribbling. Everywhere, ball point pens were scratching out memoranda explaining exactly why the client should do, or not do, something based on the law and the facts. But at my table, to my deep chagrin, I heard not the sound of scribbling, but the sound of pages flipping. "Flip, flip . .

. flip . . . flip, flip." My neighbor was flipping pages, attempting to make sense of the task at hand, and her pen was high in the air (I imagined), nowhere near the page where it might spill ink and gather points. "Here comes Number Five," I thought, with not a little sadness for my neighbor.

Incidentally, that experience fuels my writing of this book. If I can reach just one person and help them through the practical test, and enable them to put the pen on the page (or the fingers on the keyboard), maybe, just maybe, they can break on through to the other side of the bar exam, and serve our fellow citizens as an Attorney at Law . . .

Accordingly, throughout your practical test, glance at the time (and not your neighbor) to ensure that you will complete your answer on time. Work during your practice tests to leave yourself plenty of time to organize and write your answer.

H. Practice, Practice, Practice

How do you get good at practical tests? You do them! And then you look at model answers to see if you are close. At first, you might have to peek a bit at model answers, especially if the massive amount of information in the library overwhelms. But as you practice, you will see that each document in the library compliments the others, and they all fit together like a puzzle. Once you have sharpened your practical test-taking skills, you do not need to keep hammering away at them. Do a timed test or two so you get the sensation of meeting the time limit with a solid answer, and then turn to other time intensive tasks such as learning substantive law and practicing essays and multiple-choice questions. Take a practical test perhaps once or twice more as February or July lengthens. Even though the practical test may count for a quarter of your score on the bar exam, you do not need to spend one quarter of your preparation time and effort on mastering the practical test.

I. Concise Instructions for the Practical Test

Know the structure of the exam before Exam Day.

Write your answer in the correct booklet/place.

Manage your time – save 2/3 of your time for actual writing.

Identify the task to be performed.

Read the library thoroughly.

Outline your answer using AIRAC.

Confirm you are performing the correct task.

Write your answer.

Quote the rules from the library, and cite it as legal authority.

Address every element of the rules (All Elements Rule).

Use all of the evidence from the library (All Evidence Suggestion).

Use something from every document in the library.

Compare the facts and outcomes of the cases in the library with the facts of your case.

Deal with evidentiary, jurisdictional and other auxiliary issues.

V. The Multiple-Choice Part

A. A War Story

The hardest test I ever took in my life was the 1998 United States Patent Bar Examination. The pass rate barely reached 35 %, so I Am Not Kidding when I tell you it was *hard*. The exam format was rather like the multiple-choice portion of state bar exams: a hundred multiple-choice questions over six hours with a short break in between. Significantly, the exam was open book. Still, only a third of the candidates passed. Let me tell you how I did it.

I had my trusty Manual of Patent Examining Procedure on my desk, brightly flagged with sticky tongues of plastic. I favored yellow flags because pencil writing appeared with greatest contrast on the yellow portion. The "M.P.E.P." was the size of a telephone book. (If you have never seen a telephone book, ask your grandma how big that is.) And I did not *touch* the massive tome during the exam! I am sure you know that if you are diving into your book during an open-book exam, *it is too late*. I had my trusty Number Two pencils in a plastic sandwich bag, along with a small pencil sharpener. Each pencil was slightly used, because filling in a bubble on a multiple-choice test goes faster if the pencil lead tip is slightly dull. (How did I know this? Practice tests!) Those pencils became my lucky talisman on all future bar exams, and I have lent them to others for their bar exams, LSAT tests, SAT and ASVAB tests. The repeated successes add to the pencil's mystical powers. Sitting here today, I can still smell the woody aroma of those pencils ready to take that exam.

The exam was difficult to say the least. I battled through the first half that morning, and ate my sandwich with friends at lunch. Our nervous banter gave way to the afternoon struggle. I slogged through grueling questions for almost three more hours to reach the home stretch. Ten minutes were left, and a dozen questions remained untouched. I turned the page, and to my surprise, the fact pattern for the next question was *massive*. Most questions were about two thirds of a column long, and two questions appeared on a page. But not this behemoth! It sprawled all the way down the first column, and half-way down the second. I flipped the page. Another monster! I flipped more pages, and there were *five beastly questions in a row!* Mercifully, I found the last few questions were of average length. I dove into those questions, blasting through the short fact patterns and selecting the best answers my tired brain could seize. I was *very careful* to mark the answer bubble on my answer sheet next to the number of the question I was answering. Two minutes remained. I turned back to the five massive questions.

My blood ran cold. There was no way I could even *read* one fact pattern in the time left. I scanned the answers, and Answer E stated "All of the above," indicating that Answers A, B, C, and D were all correct answers to the question. With fatalistic calm washing over me, I marked "E." I had nothing to lose, and there was no way I could discern a better answer before time was up. I turned the page. Answer E for the next question was "None of the above." I furiously marked E with my very-dull pencil. Turned the page. Answer E said something about "...the above." Answer E got filled in. Flip! I noted the word "above" in the brief answer next to the letter E, so again I marked "E." The final monster fact pattern emerged into view on the next page, and I marked Answer E before even noticing that Answer E related to the "above" Answers A through D. "Time!" bellowed the proctor, and my pencil rose from the page. My hand trembled ever so slightly, and my weary eyes regarded the string of black pearls down the "E" column on my answer sheet. I was done.

Because I had completed a number of practice exams beforehand, I estimated that I scored right around 70 % on the real exam. And passing required 70 %, so I was on pins and needles wondering if I would have to take the bastard again.

Months later, the answers were published, and I learned I had passed. Many friends were not so fortunate (I worked in a large patent law firm then, and we newbies all studied for it together). I tore through the answers and found that **ONE** of the monster questions had a correct answer of E. I warmed with satisfaction, knowing that my desperate grab at Answer E got me one more correct answer. And to this day, I am sure that single correct answer put me over the top to pass the Hardest Test I Ever Took.

B. Studying for a Multiple-Choice Exam

In my view, studying for a multiple-choice test requires almost more practice than internalization. But it does require internalization. Besides, each subject on the multiple-choice exam appears on the essay exam, and could appear in the practical test. So do not forget your internalization.

Briefly, do the same things to internalize, to study, for a multiple-choice test as you would do for the essay exam. Outline, or prepare flash cards, or whatever works for you.

C. Practicing for a Multiple-Choice Exam

Honestly, though, by far the most effective way to study for the multiple-choice portion of the bar exam is to read a practice question, struggle to identify the correct answer, and then look up the correct answer. Go back to the question and reason out why the right answer is the right answer. Early in your approach to a new subject, also look up the black letter law that governs the question.

Patterns will emerge. You will read a question, and intuitively you will begin to sense the call of the question. What are they looking for? If you do enough practice questions, you will become very good at recognizing those patterns. And, a bonus effect will be enjoyed on Exam Day: You will see the *same questions* again! It is very easy to struggle with a question before the exam, learn the right answer and why, and then see the same question again. Easy points! But always read the question very carefully! A “not” changes the question 180 degrees, as does a change from “The defendant is *guilty* because . . ." to "The defendant is *acquitted* because . . .." I saw substantially the same question maybe one-in-twenty questions, because I did **a lot** of practice questions (you should too!).

Here's how to attack a multiple-choice question:

Read the question (not the fact pattern) first, to know what the question seeks.

Read, or skim, the answer choices to know what the answer will look like.

Read the fact pattern carefully.

Read the question again.

Read the answer choices carefully.

Eliminate the two wrong answers.

Make the best choice between the two remaining answers.

Mark the answer on the question AND on the answer sheet.

Okay, let's work through an example.

> Johnny was walking his pet lion, named Leo, down the sidewalk one day. He had the lion on a leash, and

carried with him an electric stun gun. Johnny and Leo encountered George walking toward them on the sidewalk. When George saw Johnny and Leo, George continued walking toward them and did not cross the street. Leo suddenly escaped Johnny's control and attacked George. Johnny was unable to control Leo or stop the attack even using the stun gun on Leo. Leo bit George, causing injury.

Johnny is liable to George for his injury caused by Leo because:

A. Johnny failed to act as a holder in due course in controlling Leo.

B. George was not contributorily negligent.

C. Leo violated George's Fourth Amendment rights.

D. Johnny is strictly liable.

First, read the question. That is the sentence (or fragment thereof) right before the lettered answer choices. "Johnny is liable to George for his injury caused by Leo because:" That tells you a wealth of information. We are looking for a reason to find Johnny liable. Someone (something) named Leo did the injury, and someone named George got the worst of it. Incidentally, the question further informs you this is probably a torts question because of the words "liable" and "injury." Now skim the answers. Answer A is probably not the right answer, because "holder in due course" is not a tort doctrine. If you are confident that A is a ridiculous choice, put a light pencil mark through "A," so you do not waste time reading Answer A again. Answer B looks good, because contributory negligence is a tort doctrine. Answer C looks ridiculous because the Fourth Amendment does not relate to tort liability. But keep an open mind – we haven't read the fact pattern yet. (What if Leo is a police dog, and Johnny a cop?) Answer D looks good right now, at least because strict liability also is a tort theory.

Now read the fact pattern carefully. (I will pause while you read.) Okay, we got a pet lion, Johnny the owner, George the victim. Johnny took all those precautions to control the lion, namely the leash and the stun gun, but the lion still attacked. Read the question again carefully. Johnny is liable. Why? Read the answer choices carefully. There was no unlawful search and seizure, so Answer C can be crossed off for sure now. Answer A remains ridiculous, too, although now you see the humor – Johnny was holding the leash, but that did not make him a holder in due course. Light pencil marks through "A" and "C" indicate that you have eliminated the two wrong answers.

Now you have to pick between Answer B and Answer D. This is where the question separates Attorneys at Law from People Who Just Watch Court TV. Answer B says that George was not contributorily negligent. Note in the fact pattern that "George continued walking toward them and did not cross the street." (Hey, if I saw a lion walking toward me, even if he was on a leash, I am not sure I would just keep walking Right Into The Jaws Of Death! Reasonable people find a way to avoid the lion, right?) But George had every right to be on the sidewalk. He pays his taxes (we may presume), and could reasonably assume that someone walking a lion on a sidewalk would have control over the big cat. So Answer B looks pretty good, right? But Answer B is incorrect.

Answer D is correct because you previously read, outlined, or flashcarded the rule that "exotic or wild animals carry strict liability for their owners." Or you learn it when you look up the right answer to the question. It matters not whether Johnny was negligent when strict liability controls. If Johnny's negligence does not come into play, George's *contributory negligence* is irrelevant as well. Answer D is the best choice as between Answer B and Answer D, therefore.

Put a dash next to Answer B and circle Answer D. Do this so that you can be certain that you have marked your answer next to the right number on your answer sheet. Also, the dash tells you that Answer B was the Least Ridiculous Answer among the wrong answers, if you have time to come back and review the question. You could evaluate whether Answer B or Answer

D is correct, if you still have doubt. More good practices appear below.

D. Good Test Taking Practices

There are many beautiful things about a multiple-choice test. First, the right answer is already on the page. Second, if you have no clue about a question, it is just one teeny tiny little question on a great big exam. You don't even have to answer that question and you will still pass the bar exam. Third, when you complete the multiple-choice portion of the bar exam, you are done! No more pencils, no more books, no more bar examiner's dirty looks!

During the test, note the start time so you can gauge the end time. It can make a huge difference if the test started at 9:00 AM or 9:10 AM. That knowledge will mean a lot to you at about 11:55 AM, and you have eight questions left. Do you have just five minutes left in the test? Or are you aware that you have fifteen minutes, until 12:10 PM?

Mark your answers in your test booklet. Use a system, so you know what your marks mean. Above, I suggested crossing out the letters of the ridiculous answers, or the answers you know are wrong. Put a dash next to the least ridiculous answer, and circle the letter of the answer you determine to be correct. Circling the correct answer will save your mind, heart, general overall health, and your Lawyer Candidacy when you glance back from time to time to ensure that you are marking the answers next to the correct numbers on the answer sheet. Be careful to avoid any appearance of cheating. Shield your test booklet (and your answer sheet) so your fellow lawyer candidates cannot see your answers. Avoid any appearance of impropriety. You do not want to have to explain your innocence when the exam proctor catches your neighbor repeatedly looking your way.

Mark your answers clearly on your answer sheet. Start with a slightly-dull pencil, and fill in the bubble completely. Do not place incomplete marks on your answer sheet with the idea that you will come back to fill in the bubbles. (What if they call time before you fill in those bubbles?) Fill in each bubble *as you go*. It is a correct answer in the bag, and you never have to mess with it again.

Mark your answer next to the correct number. Seriously. I have heard sob stories where people taking multiple-choice tests skipped a line, or placed two answers on the same line, and then every subsequent answer appeared next to an incorrect number. *The horror!* Freak out about this now. (I will pause while you freak out.) But don't make that mistake on Exam Day!

I offer two techniques for avoiding marking the answer next to the wrong number.

First, circle your answer in your test booklet. Then, from time to time, spot-check your answer sheet. "Question 27 – I marked 'A' in my test booklet. On my answer sheet, next to '27,' I see 'A' marked." Do that once every ten or thirty minutes. If you do The Bad, Bad Thing, do not panic.

Your answers are circled in your test booklet, so you can readily find where your answer sheet got off track and fix it. It is worth the few minutes it would take to correct your answer sheet, because you already worked hard to cipher the correct answers. Now go get credit for them! The question or two you might have to skip later in the test, just guess at an answer if you must.

Second, when you determine the correct answer, say to yourself the question number AND the correct answer. "47 is B." Then, place your finger on "47" on your answer sheet, and fill in bubble "B." Repeat to yourself, "47 is B." Then look back at your test booklet on your way to Question 48, and confirm that for Question 47, you have circled Answer B. "Yep. 47 is B." Of course, do NOT use your outside-your-head voice when doing that.

Mark an answer for every question. As you can see in my War Story above, it got me another point, even though I had no hope of comprehending the question in the time I had left. As you keep track of your time, note when you have only a few minutes left. Then pick a letter and mark away for every unanswered question you have left. I think it is best to pick just one letter, than to randomly mark letters. If you go with one letter, chances are decent that you will get every one-in-four correct. I favor the letter "C." I picked Answer E on the Patent Bar Exam just because of the "all of the above," "none of the above" format of Answer E for those monster questions.

Circle, or place a star or other mark, in your test booklet next to the number of the questions that trouble you. Then, if you finish with time left, go back through your test booklet looking for those trouble questions. Attack the question again, and see if you calmly and rationally arrive at a different answer. If you remain unsure, and cannot pick between the two best answers, leave the question and move on. Or, if you become certain of one answer, mark your answer sheet accordingly.

If you finish with time left, look at your answer sheet. Have you answered every question? Have you filled in the right bubbles completely? Spot check against your test booklet to ensure that the circled answers are marked on your answer sheet. Erase fully any answers that you marked and then changed. Also erase completely any stray pencil marks on your answer sheet. Make sure your identification appears filled in correctly on your answer sheet. Now smile, Counselor: **You have finished the bar exam!**

VI. What to Expect on Exam Day

A. To Write, or to Type?

Back in my day (insert geezer cough here), the vast majority of lawyer candidates wrote the essays by hand. However, we had a choice whether we would write the bar exam essays by hand, or type it out on our laptops. Those who applied and were allowed to type their essays were placed in a separate room so that the deafening sound of their fingers pounding away on keyboards would not distract those of us furiously scribbling. (A thousand people scribbling can form a pretty impressive sound, too.)

If you strongly prefer one format over the other, pay attention to how and when you must select your desired format. You may have to request that format as early as when you first apply to sit for the bar exam. If you want to type, make sure that you refresh your laptop with any necessary software updates, you have properly downloaded the software for the bar exam, and your laptop functions perfectly. The exam proctors will be sympathetic to you on Exam Day if you are having a malfunction, but they might not have the time or the talent to sort out why your laptop does not want to cooperate. Be prepared to write out your essays as a Back-Up Plan.

The software the bar will ask you to download isolates your screen from the rest of your laptop's memory and storage to prevent cheating. That software allows you to type up your essays and submit them in a secure, identifiable way, while making anything else stored on your laptop inaccessible while the exam software runs. Even so, avoid having anything on your laptop on Exam Day that could be misconstrued as material useful for cheating. You just do not want to have to explain why your secured transactions outline rests undeleted in your Recycle Bin. Avoid the appearance of impropriety.

If you decide to write your essays by hand, select a useful pen. To do that, I purchased booklets containing the same relatively flimsy paper that the actual exam booklets would contain, and I tested a number of pens on that paper. I tested which pens wrote well, and which pens' ink did not bleed through the paper. I favored Pilot V-Ball pens with "fine" tips (0.5 mm) and blue ink. "Medium" tips (0.7 mm) and "wide" tips (1.0 mm) bled through – I saved those luxurious ink bleeders for signing my name to all those lawyer letters I was going to write after I passed the bar. When practicing, use actual booklets at least once to familiarize yourself with size limitations and mechanics of writing in those booklets.

Write double space. Leave a space in between your writing. This does a couple of things. First, and very importantly, it makes your essay easier to read. It may even improve your handwriting. Second, it gives you a chance to insert a sentence. In my experience, bar examiners do not mind the occasional additional thought. However, if your whole essay appears chaotically disorganized, that is Not A Good Thing.

Write legibly. Practice, and make the effort to really make each word legible. Some abbreviations are okay, but do not write your essay with the same grammar with which you text your friends. (I recall vividly Prof. Freer warning us in his Bar/Bri® lecture on civil procedure to spell out the word "question" in lieu of a question mark as an abbreviation, so the bar examiners do not read your issue statement as, "This is a federal?")

Practice should help you decide whether to write or to type. (Do this before it is too late to change your choice with the bar!) If you write illegibly, then type. If you type way too slowly, then write! Let me teach you a hint about typing, if you never took a typing class: the "F" key and the "J" key have little ridges on them so you can re-orient your hands without looking at the keyboard. (As I type that, I have to admit that I do not use those ridges. Instead, I look at the screen and use that to orient my hands. If I type gibberish, my fingers are hitting the wrong keys.)

B. Travel to the Bar Exam

Woody Allen said 80 % of life is showing up. Someone else said, "99 % of life is showing up *prepared*." Fair enough. I say, "100 % of the people who pass the bar exam show up *well practiced*." I digress. Please show up to the bar exam. I urge you to secure hotel accommodations in the town where the exam will take place long before the exam itself. Everybody and their grandmother will also stay in town those days. Get a hotel room as close to the exam venue as possible, hopefully so you can walk, especially if parking will be problematic. If you must drive, reduce your keys to the bare essentials. You don't want that fancy key fob to raise suspicions. I am serious.

Get to town at least a day early, two if you can swing it. Acclimatize yourself to your room, the town, the weather. Award yourself bonus points if someone else will drive you, if driving is necessary. You can continue to study along the way, or rest, even if you are not asleep.

On Exam Day, get there reasonably early. You do not want the stress of traffic to damage the aura of prepared confidence that you will exude that morning. It is better to arrive early, get registered, and get seated than to have to run in late and risk the exam proctors telling you to go home because the exam has already begun.

C. Sleep, Nutrition, and Hydration

I know the bar exam represents, shall we say, an exciting time. Your desire to cram it all in may tempt you to cut back or skip sleep. This is not a law school fun run one-hour exam that you could cram for the night before. You must take care of your body and your mind, and be prepared to endure two or three days of testing. That requires sleep.

I would urge you to avoid drugs, especially drugs that you have not used before or don't use regularly. No, I don't mean heroin and cocaine drugs. I mean caffeine and sleep aids. If you do not know how your body will react, the night before Exam Day is no time to experiment. Being too juiced on caffeine or too groggy from a sleeping pill might throw you off your game. For a mild stimulant, go for a walk or a run. To sleep better at night, go for a walk or run early the day before. Having said that, if you have a coffee habit, for example, please by all means continue. Just don't overdo it. The adrenaline will carry you pretty far anyway.

As Exam Day gets closer, regulate your nutrition and hydration to give you three-hour periods each morning and each afternoon where you do not need food, water, or a bathroom break. Train your body by blocking out those times from 9:00 AM to noon, and from 1:00 PM to 4:00 PM, and avoiding sustenance during those times. Practice also eating a light lunch only, so that you do not have food coma during the afternoon.

I believe that one of my four bar exams allowed us to bring a bottle of water. I cannot recall which one. Was it South Carolina? We had nicely air-conditioned rooms at the state fairgrounds in Columbia. Was it Virginia? Could have been. We took the test in a large ballroom of a fancy hotel in Richmond. I am pretty sure it was not allowed for the DC bar exam. There, the test was administered in several rooms of a public library or a school – funny how I can't recall exactly. (That's what I want for you: that the Bar Exam is a vague contented memory in your distant past!) I remember the patent bar exam allowed us to bring a sandwich in a clear sandwich bag, but we could not touch it until lunchtime. In any case, know exactly what you are allowed to bring in the way of snacks and beverages, and train your body to conform to what you can bring in the week or so leading up to Exam Day.

D. What You Can Bring; What You Cannot Bring

You can bring only what the bar says you can bring. Read those instructions carefully, and do not goof it up. Anything that you bring that is not allowed, be ready to trash it or put it in your car during the exam. Make sure your laptop is fully charged; the exam proctors may provide an electrical outlet for you to charge your laptop during the exam.

Definitely bring pens and pencils (sharpened, but slightly dull). Bring your laptop preloaded with the software for taking the bar exam. The Virginia bar examiners insisted that everything we brought fit into a clear sandwich bag (except for the laptop), so our full possessions could be readily examined for contraband. That list included: an identification, a registration document, six pens, six pencils, and keys. An analogue watch. Oh yeah, medication if you had a doctor's note and cleared it ahead of time. Whew. That's it.

The Virginia bar exam also required us to dress like lawyers – suits and ties for the guys, equivalent for the girls – but also insisted on soft-soled shoes so you wouldn't disturb others if you had to get up and walk around. Imagine a thousand lawyer candidates in suits, dresses, and tennis shoes! My point: know your dress code, if there is one, for the bar exam.

E. Watch Your Time, and Follow Directions

I know I have said it before, but it is worth saying it again. Lawyer candidates, smart people, get defeated on the bar exam by simple mechanics. They skip a multiple-choice question, and then complete an entire column of questions before they realize that they are marking their answers on the wrong row. And they are unable to see where they began this awful mistake. The whole answer sheet becomes suspect. Or, in their haste, they have written the family law essay in the secured transactions answer booklet. Because the booklet does not mention "holder in due course" anywhere, the bar examiner cannot award a single point. *And watch your time.* I am sure you can write a better answer if you have an hour per question; unfortunately, you only have thirty minutes.

Following directions also means avoiding disqualification. Make certain that you give the exam proctors no reason to throw you out of the bar exam, or to suspect you of cheating. Don't open your packet until they tell you to. Don't flip over the fact pattern until they tell you to. The exam proctors are not brutal horrible people, but if you cannot follow their instructions, they have no choice but to act accordingly. Further, they cannot let one lawyer candidate disrupt the bar exam for all of the other candidates. I have seen it where someone opened the packet too soon – the exam proctors corrected the candidate and the candidate rapidly flipped over the documents so nothing could be read. It was clear to all that nerves, and not mischievous intent, caused the packet to open early, so the candidate suffered no other consequence. Finally, stop when time is called. If you have a chance, put a period on the page as your pen lifts in the air – like you meant to end it that way! Seeking one more point is not worth risking total disqualification.

VII. Final Word of Encouragement

Remember, Dear Reader, this is a marathon, not a sprint. It is a marathon both in the sense that you have a lot of work to do in the next two months, and in the sense that two or three days of testing will require stamina and endurance. Accordingly, you need to take care of yourself mentally and physically. And emotionally and spiritually, for that matter. Let's talk physical. You must eat right, with a variety of foods in sufficient amount. Sure, indulge a little with junk food and caffeine if you like (I hit some coffee ice cream when I was studying for my first bar exam – how's that for killing two birds with one stone!). Avoid stress eating, though. You must get sufficient sleep, of course. I strongly urge you to exercise in accordance with your current state of fitness. Walking or running gets you some fresh air and keeps your metabolism going. Go for a walk once a day and/or a run every other day (of course, after you have consulted with your fave health care provider). Exercise releases endorphins that give you a sense of well-being, so use that to combat negative feelings during your preparation. Keep in touch with your significant other, your mom, your dad, your besties, your classmates, whomever, to provide you that emotional grounding. *You can do this,* and they can help. Study groups also help, but use them to encourage one another, and do not let them devolve into freak-out sessions, nor let them distract you from studying with a false sense of effective effort. Exchange and constructively critique practice essays and practical test answers. Stay spiritually nurtured too. I have heard it said that prayer will never be abolished from public schools until they do away with pop quizzes. And so it is among lawyer candidates so long as there are bar exams. Praise the Lord and pass the Number Two pencils!

If you have any feedback, war stories, criticisms, or victory speeches, please e-mail me at DrStipkala@gmail.com. And I really want to hear your victory speech, Counselor! What helped you pass the bar exam? What did not help so much? How can we help future lawyer candidates enjoy a more effective bar exam preparation experience? I ask for your feedback because being a lawyer is really about helping others, serving others. As your First Act as a Successful Lawyer Candidate and Conqueror Of The Bar Exam, help me help others with your feedback. I and they would be most grateful!

Made in the USA
Monee, IL
04 November 2026

67391351R00079